BLACK LIKE WHO?

BLACK LIKE WHO?

Writing · Black · Canada

by Rinaldo Walcott

a misFit
b o o k

INSOMNIAC PRESS

Edited by Michael Holmes/a misFit book
Copy edited by Lloyd Davis & Liz Thorpe
Designed by Mike O'Connor
a misFit book logo designed by D.A. Holmes

Canadian Cataloguing in Publication Data

Walcott, Rinaldo, 1965-
    Black like who?

Includes bibliographical references and index.
ISBN 1-895837-07-3

1. Black Canadians. 2. Blacks - Canada. 3. Blacks -
    Canada - Race identity. I. Title.

FC106.B6W34 1997   305.896'071   C97-931373-2
F1035.N3W34 1997

The publisher gratefully acknowledges the support of the Ontario Arts Council

Printed and bound in Canada

Insomniac Press, 378 Delaware Ave.
Toronto, Ontario, Canada, M6H 2T8

Acknowledgements

The essays collected here are representative of what it means to live the in-between and not to be troubled by the life of the in-between. I wish to thank many people who have contributed to the development of my thoughts about modes of address and the politics of blackness in Canada. First, despite, and in spite of, my dedication of this book to Kasia Rukszto and Kass Banning, I want to thank them both again for encouraging me to think and write about black Canadian "things". This book exists because of them. Over the last few years my life of the mind has been enriched by the friendship of Deborah Britzman, Daniel Yon, Warren Crichlow, Alice Pitt, Maryjo Nadeau, Gamal Abdel-Shehid, Robert Gill, Cynthia Wright and, last but not least, Leslie Sanders. Other people have played an important role in my thinking about blackness as both a category and a sign, its performativity: Honor Ford Smith, Winston Smith, Russell Chace and many others have provided me with reading materials and questions to consider. I also want to thank Michael Holmes for approaching me with this project and having faith in it from its tiniest beginning. Not many people are interested in black Canadian work and the imprint "a misFit book" clearly is appropriate. I want to thank Lynn Crosbie for introducing us. I also want to acknowledge and thank Mike O'Connor of Insomniac Press for a rather pleasurable publishing experience. Finally, I thank my sister Aurelia Best, who was the first to teach me the things which might yet make a good thinker of me: the ability to question and to read, read, read — thank you. The flaws, weaknesses and follies are all mine.

Some of these essays have had a life of their own. I am grateful to the publishers for allowing me to reprint them, even though they are all very different from their initial appearance. *CineAction* 39 (1995), *Pictures of a Generation on Hold: Selected Papers*, edited by M. Pomerance and J. Sakeris (Toronto: Media Studies Working Group, 1996), *Westcoast Line 22* (31/1: Spring-Summer 1997) and a plethora of conferences have visited these texts.

For Kasia and Kass,

your insistence is grace

A note on the cover photograph

The photograph was taken in 1905 at the first Niagara Movement meeting (it eventually became a part of the National Association for the Advancement of Colored People [NAACP]) held in Niagara Falls, Ontario. The American side of the Falls was painted into the background of the photo. The 1905 meeting could not find the time nor space to enter into dialogue and conversation with black Canadians. Yet Canada was the only place these African-American radicals could find overnight shelter. The photo represents many of the ironies, exchanges and absences which characterize black histories and contemporary life. One obvious and glaring example is the absence of women in the picture, despite their presence and participation at the meeting. This book is both a homage to those moments of black diasporic relations and a reminder that we must not romanticize those moments but critically reflect upon and engage with them instead.

I would like to gratefully acknowledge The Schomburg Center for Research in Black Studies at the New York Public Library for allowing us to reproduce the cover photograph.

Table of Contents

Introduction:
Writing Blackness After...

Writing blackness is difficult work. The sliding signifier of blackness intends to continue to slide and remain out of bounds. And that is a good thing. Yet to read blackness as merely "playful" is to fall into a wilful denial of what it means to live "black". In the chapters that follow I attempt to pay attention to what is at stake in thinking about blackness and its cultural, political and social performativity both in Canada and beyond its borders. The ideas here are neither unique nor new; instead, they insist upon bringing a careful eye to what happens here. Black Canadian culture would do well to have its critics grow up right along with it. Peering into the works of black Canadian artists allows for a confrontation with the complexities of black life and identifications, while still being aware of black "imitative" and derivative practices. However, it seems to be the critic's job to tease out what is "imitation" or copy and what is (re)invention. My discussion of mimesis and alterity in the poetic works of Dionne Brand and M. Nourbese Philip, therefore, is an attempt to question and figure out the difference between the original, the copy and the "new". I suggest that the appearance of sameness or mimetic practices in their poetic works actually announces their alterity, their difference, and possibly their "newness".

Furthermore, I suggest that it is useful to read black Canadian works within the context of black diasporic discourses. Those who are descendants of Africans (New World Blacks) dispersed by TransAtlantic slavery continue to engage in a complex process of cultural exchange, invention and (re)invention, and the result is cultural creolization. In most of the chapters that follow questions of diasporic aesthetics, borrowing, and sharing are discussed. These issues are explored not in a romantic fashion, but as both a necessity of life and, sometimes, a limitation on politics. In particular my critique of Stephen Williams's and Clement Virgo's feature films raises the question of borrowing without the process for (re)invention. My critique of the derivative nature and limitations of both films is, therefore, an indication of where a too- easy diasporic gesture fails. If I suggest anything in the following pages, it is that black diasporic cultures are most engaging and critically affirmative when the practices of (re)invention are highlighted and displayed in a complex fashion.

In some of the essays I suggest that music and other imaginative works best demonstrate the processes of black diasporic invention and (re)invention. I argue that these works often offer complex analyses of black performativity and therefore of black political identifications. Additionally, I suggest that these works are not merely national products, but that they occupy the space of the in-between, vacillating between national borders and diasporic desires, ambitions and disappointments. These works suggest the possibilities of the "new", but in many cases can not leave various kinds of "old" behind.

The chapters in this book initially were all written as separate essays, and continue to bear the marks of their individuality. Yet these essays speak to the problem of writing blackness in Canada as they simultaneously represent the problem. The chapters concentrate mainly, but not exclusively, on black cultures in Ontario, and therefore can not adequately account for black cultures in other parts of Canada. Yet I would argue that it is not so much local culture that is my focus, but rather the expansive questions that are posed. Therefore, we might think of the method used as one where local cultures beget expansive questions. Any omissions are therefore not considered as unworthy of study but rather represent my preoccupations at a particular time and place. Here's my disclaimer: Do not read this book as a treatise on blackness in Canada. Instead, read the essays as an attempt to articulate some grammars for thinking Canadian blackness.

Writing blackness after the civil-rights era, second wave feminism, black cultural nationalism, gay and lesbian liberation, the Clarence Thomas/Anita Hill spectacle, the Rodney King beating and L.A. riots, the Yonge Street Riots, and the O.J. Simpson trials, is difficult work. Yet, writing blackness remains important work. Black postmodernity insists upon being chronicled as it makes fun of and spoofs the very notion of writing blackness. A certain kind of upheaval of "blacknesses" exists which makes apparent the senselessness of writing blackness even as we are compelled and forced to write it.

In a Canadian context, writing blackness is a scary scenario: we are an absented presence always under erasure. Located between the U.S. and the Caribbean, Canadian blackness is a bubbling brew of desires for elsewhere, disappointments in the nation and the pleasures of exile — even for those who have resided here for many generations. The project of articulating Canadian blackness is difficult not because of the small number of us trying to take the tentative steps towards writing it, but rather because of the ways in which so many of us are nearly always preoccupied with elsewhere and very seldom with here. It seems then that a tempered arrogance might be a necessary element of any grammar that is used to construct a language for writing blackness in Canada. A shift in gaze can be an important moment.

The writing of blackness in Canada, then, might begin with a belief that something important happens here. If we accept this, finally, then critics can move beyond mere celebration into the sustaining work that critique is. A belief that something important happens here would mean that celebration could become the site for investigating ourselves in critical ways. We can begin to refuse the seductions of "firstness" and engage in critique, dialogue and debate, which are always much more sustaining than celebrations of originality. The essays in this book attempt to engage the project of recognizing that something important does happen here.

Finally, I would like to end this introduction with a note on language. Throughout the essays I use the terms blackness and black Canadian. I do not use the term African-Canadian, because I think of it as a borrowing from the African-American context, one that needs to be better thought through. African-Canadian and African-American carry with them a particular connotation which is very much related to distancing oneself from the black urban poor and working class. Forms of naming based on ethnicity are often deployed in an attempt to deny the complexity of what might and might not constitute blackness.

Similarly, when I use the term blackness, I mean to signal blackness as a sign, one that carries with it particular histories of resistance and domination. But blackness is also a sign which is never closed and always under contestation.

Blackness for me, like black Canadian, allows for a certain kind of malleability and open-endedness which means that questions of blackness far exceed the categories of the biological and the ethnic. I deploy blackness as a discourse, but that discourse is embedded in a history or a set of histories which are messy and contested. The essays that follow demonstrate how various kinds of blackness are always in progress, always in the process of becoming...

"Going to the North"
The Limit of Black Diasporic Discourse(s)

We are all jogging,
Jog, jog, jogging,
And we're all jogging
We are going to the North
(Delany 142)

This is a meditation on the place of black Canadas[1] in contemporary discourses of black diaspora(s) and the black
Atlantic. I do not seek to promulgate a simple notion of
inclusion for such is no longer necessary, sufficient nor
required — black Canadas exist and will continue to do so.[2]
Instead I mean to attend to the spaces or gaps through which
our current thinking of diaspora might receive continued
invigoration if a detour is taken via or through Canada. Such
a detour has been well-established for African-Americans by
conversations which make the Underground Railroad central
to questions of "freedom".

My detours are historical and contemporary, literary and
musical, popular and not. I use detour as a method for thinking through the circuitous routes of black diasporic cultures,
their connectedness and differences. Detours are the

(un)acknowledged routes and roots of black expressive cultures and gestures directly to their rhizomatic nature. The detour is both an improvisatory and an in-between space which black diasporic cultures occupy. Detours, both planned and accidental, are an important aspect of black diasporic cultures. The first detour might be considered Columbus'; it set the groundwork for discussions of blackness in the Americas.

I take my incitement from the way Paul Gilroy traverses the black Atlantic. His insistence on reading and adding Europe and black Britain into the texture of arguments and debates concerning intellectual property and ethnic absolutism in the diaspora is of importance to my project. Given this, I am also interested in entering into dialogue with Gilroy's assertion that other travels need to be mapped and charted. If the ship is Gilroy's metaphor for the black Atlantic, the vehicle in which he travels and docks at the doorstep of African-Americans, then for overland travel, jogging might be the metaphor that best characterizes the back and forth movement of black Canada and its offerings to the discourse of diaspora.

When a group of African-Americans met in Fort Erie, Ontario, in 1905 under the banner of the Niagara Movement, with W.E.B. DuBois as their main organizer and leader, the location of the meeting was not occasioned by choice, but by the inability to find lodgings on the American side of the border, where they were residents. The Niagara Movement, which eventually became the NAACP, did not invite black Canadians to be a part of their meetings. Despite this exclusion, blacks in Canada attempted to enter into dialogue with the organizers of the inaugural meeting.[3] The fact that many of the "Canadian" blacks who would have gladly participated in the inaugural meeting were born in America, or were immediate descendants of African-American slaves who had escaped to Canada, makes this exclusion interesting. A refusal to acknowledge black Canadians in this first instance might be construed as the historical limit of the current discourse of diaspora, as it is being formulated and reformulated, in the two contexts that I am interested in — black studies and black cultural studies.

This moment of exclusion should not be taken lightly in terms of historical interpretations of how porous the Canada-United States border remains for diasporic blacks and what kinds of political identifications and relationships are possible. That Canada existed as an ambivalent place of "freedom" for African-Americans is just one of the ideas which need to be considered in light of current debates. The creation of the League for the Advancement of Coloured People[4] by black Canadians is an important moment of cross-border political identification. Such identifications are suggestive of the relations of diasporic communicative acts and outer-national practices and desires. Nonetheless, the ethnic particularity of African-Americans might be questioned in terms of political organization for its oversight in refusing to dialogue with black folks within the host borders of the first NAACP meeting. The significance of this can not be overlooked given the current contestations over theories of diaspora, the black Atlantic, and thus black studies and black cultural studies.

I address an amalgam of practices which speak to both the possibilities and limits of theorizing diaspora as a way to pose the question of what is at stake in this postmodern, transglobal world, when some aspects of the nation-state remain firmly in place for the unruly, resistant citizens located on the inside/outside axis of a given nation. My intentions are to attend to a number of conversations which deploy and make use of diaspora, black studies and (black) cultural studies as a way of conceiving a conversation that exceeds national boundaries. I am particularly concerned about what Paul Gilroy has termed "ethnic absolutism".

Now it is clear that any conversation about blackness that attempts to bring a discussion of Canada to the table is hampered by two primary problems: the proximity to and influence on Canada of America, one of the most powerful capitalist and imperialist nations; and the dominance and impact of American cultural production on Canada. I am suggesting that the effect is not only Americanization, as Canadian nationalists would have it. These two factors actually create something that is not merely a politics of exclusion; rather they can foster a retreat to discourses of nationalism which become short-sighted in terms of the transnational political identifications that might be crucially necessary in our times. In the case of black folks, a diasporic connectedness and intimacy is at stake. Given this, I want to take another detour deeper into the historical records.

In *Condition, Elevation, Emigration and Destiny of the Coloured People of the United States*, Martin Robinson Delany revealed his fear and fascination with the potentialities of Canada, and argued that it was one of the best places for black people to escape to, until a national homeland was possible. Delany's ambivalence towards Canada was articulated through what he believed to be not only Canada's possible annexation by the United States, but also what was seen by him as "a manifest tendency on the part of Canadians generally, to Americanism" (174). Delany's ambivalence is astutely couched in his observations of Canadian subservience to Americans. It was on this basis that he was convinced and "satisfied that the Canadas are no place of safety for the colored people of the United States; otherwise we should have no objection to them" (176).

However, Delany continued to advocate and "promote"

Canada as an interim or provisional place where "freedom" might be had until the possibility of something "somewhere else" arose. He suggested that, "[f]reedom, always; liberty any place and ever—before slavery. Continue to fly to the Canadas, and swell the number of the twenty-five thousand already there" (177). Now to think of Delany's suggestion here as merely immigrationist is to not fully consider Delany's own "exile" in Chatham, Ontario.[5]

Some attention to the role that place and the potentialities of "freedom" in Canada might have had on Delany is useful. By no means do I want to suggest that "freedom" was had in Canada. Rather, the conditions for procuring "freedom" were much more evident (t)here. Chatham was a hotbed of anti-slavery activity, populated with fugitive slaves from the U.S., ex-slaves who had migrated from the Caribbean and ex-slaves from Canada.[6] Martin Delany was involved in raising funds to establish the town as a viable settlement owned and operated by its black residents.[7] He reportedly travelled to England to help raise funds for black families to buy property in the area. Delany's involvement in Chatham and the possibility of a black township should be highlighted in readings of his work which seek to account for his pan-national black politics. A consideration of the politics of Chatham might shed some light on his philosophical treatise of black nationalism. I want to suggest that the role place played was a fundamental part of Delany's articulation of a black nationalist project.

Chatham, and Delany's involvement in the community there, surely had some impact on what he imagined freed black people could accomplish. The struggle for land, schools, churches, and the building of other civil organizations in Chatham, might also be read as a part of the sojourn that is so crucially a part of the Exodus narrative which populates black nationalist articulations. And interestingly,

Delany's circumscription of the roles of women in black nationalist discourse might have been influenced by what he knew of Chatham. What I am suggesting is that Delany's crossover into Canada might have given him the opportunity to see his project partially in operation.

Mary Ann Shadd's work as an anti-slavery activist and newspaper woman is yet another part of the unfolding terrain of the criss-crossing of the Canadian-American border. The absence of these discussions from current conversations about the diaspora is crucial to theorizing and politicizing the (re)invigoration of black studies and the development of black cultural studies.[8] It is crucial because the Chatham project was significantly organized and influenced by black women with public roles in community politics.[9] As Robert Reid-Pharr suggests in a discussion of Delany and bourgeois sado-masochism, Delany's nationalist project meant "the domestication of many parts of Afro-America and the out and out excision of others" (87). Thus Delany's insistence on circumscribing the role of women to motherhood would have had much to do with what he knew of women's political work in Chatham.[10] Looking at the black Canadian context can also provide more evidence for the important public political roles of nineteenth-century black women.

However, I think that the representation of Canada is best achieved in Delany's novel *Blake; or the Huts of America*, which was written in Canada.[11] Crossings to Canada represent an ambivalence for any Canadian who must simultaneously grapple with the absented presence of slavery in official national discourses and the instances in nation-state narratives which argue that Canada's only relation to slavery was as a sanctuary for escaping African-Americans — via the Underground Railroad. This dilemma is important because the crossing has been appropriated by the nation as the source of its denial of an almost five-hundred-year black presence.

Joy Mannette, who argues for the necessity of acknowledg-
ing an historical black presence in Canada, has referred to the
agreements made by British soldiers in the fields with those
African-Americans who forsook their masters and fought
against the republicans as "treaties". Her claim that these initial, unofficial agreements were treaties is crucial for how
blacks in Canada might make claims on their localities. The
use of the word treaty is discursively, textually, and juridically
important because it challenges and speaks to early Canadian
state formation and the place of black people in it. Mannette's
assertion places blackness as central to early nation-state formation and therefore grounds the genealogy of black people
and blackness in Canada as inextricably bound to contemporary debates concerning the nation.

George Elliott Clarke, the African-Canadian poet and
scholar, states "[a]nother African-American, Delaney (sic) is, I
think, the first African-Canadian novelist" (7). Clarke goes on
to argue that Delany wrote *Blake* in Canada (7). Clarke's
argument is based upon an extension of Henry Louis Gates's
argument for an African-American literary canon. In many
ways, Clarke is also troping on Gates and gesturing, as well,
to the porousness of the Canadian-American border. What is
of interest to me is the evidence in *Blake* which suggests that
Canada represented a space of possible liberation, and what
this might mean for black diasporic conversations which have
almost nothing to say about Canada. I want to insist that the
rhizomatic black cultures of Canada have much to teach us,
especially about national policies like multiculturalism, which
support identity politics and limit political imaginings and
possibilities. Black diasporic utterances are cluttered with references to how their histories relate to other histories of black
people elsewhere.

In *Blake*, Andy, one of the slaves escaping to Canada, provides Delany with the opportunity to enter into dialogue with
the forces of racism and segregation that black people faced

in Canada. He articulates an ambivalence to Canada, one grounded in the regulatory and disciplinary state practices enforced on black people, those which gave rise to the construction of discourses of blackness in Canada — it was a place of sanctuary, but not necessarily a place where black people would actively participate in the public sphere. Delany's ambivalence in *Blake* might give us some insight into the continued outer-national political identification of black Canadians with black peoples elsewhere. He wrote:

> He knew not that some of high intelligence and educational attainments of his race residing in many parts of the Provinces, were really excluded from and practically denied their rights, and that there was no authority known to the colony to give redress and make restitution... It had never entered the poor Andy, that in going to Canada in search of freedom, he was then in a country where privileges were denied him which are common to the slave in every Southern state — the right of going into the gallery of a public building... that a few of the most respectable colored ladies of the town in Kent County... taking seats in the gallery of the court house assigned to females and other visitors, were ruthlessly taken hold of and shown down the stairway... An emotion of unutterable indignation would swell the heart of the determined slave, and almost compel him to curse the country of his adoption... But Andy was free... (153)

Delany's ambivalence to Canada as a promised land has its contemporary trajectory in Ismael Reed's *Flight to Canada*. Reed satirically rewrites the slave narrative, the desire to escape from slavery on the Underground Railroad, as a plane flight to Canada. His collapsing of past into present and vice versa signals the continuing importance of Canada as an ambivalent place in African-American historiography.

Also revealed in this passage from *Blake* are some important insights concerning the political activism of black Canadians (or should we say ex-African-Americans) who were quite involved in seeing their brothers liberated from slavery, while at the same time challenging local conditions of racism and segregation, and making demands for full citizenship. That it is a group of women who are led out of the gallery should not be interpreted as merely symbolic on Delany's part. As I suggested earlier, women played active and public roles in black Ontario communities, particularly in Chatham, where Delany lived. The most notable of those women was Mary Ann Shadd whose activism led to her founding a newspaper to better disseminate her, and the community's, political views.[12]

In *Blake*, Delany has Henry "invest a portion of the old people's money by the purchase of fifty acres of land with improvements suitable, and provide for the schooling of the children until he should otherwise order" (155). Those two issues, land ownership and schooling, led women to play active roles in the public sphere and challenge both anti-black racism and black patriarchy simultaneously. Thus, the kind of positions that Delany advocates in the conclusion of *The Conditions* cannot be separated from what he might or might not have known about women's public political work in Canada and the United States, and his desire to have that role played only by men. These kinds of positions have important consequences for black studies and black cultural studies as debates unfold over how to make sense of both paradigms.

So now let's take a detour through recent history. When black Canadians demonstrated over the staging of the musical *Showboat* at a publicly funded theatre (The North York Centre for the Performing Arts; renamed the Ford Centre for the Performing Arts),[13] their concerns and claims were dismissed by appeals to an African-American authenticity and an argument that stressed that a planned staging of the musical in New York did not spark the same kind of response.[14]

Henry Louis Gates Jr. was allegedly hired by *Showboat*'s production company (Livent) to produce educational materials on how to read the musical historically and make use of the musical in the contemporary era. What was most troubling about the entire episode was that the particular and specific local concerns of black Canadians were rendered suspect by a "public" lecture in which Gates entirely evacuated the notion of historical difference, collapsing the two nations.[15]

His use of a particular homogenizing practice of black studies and African-American authenticity to attempt to invalidate local black concerns has implications for how we conceive diasporic relations. What became obvious was that when we theorize diaspora or black Atlantic exchanges, dialogues, conversations and differences, we need to pay attention to national and other forms of institutional power. Those who make diasporic claims of understanding and intimacy need to pay attention to the specific concerns of various groups within a given nation while making their transnational argument. Still, the question is clear: Can African-Americans represent the locality of black Canadian political concerns? The answer is, it seems to me, no.

I want to suggest that the use of Gates's body, knowledge, and institutional accoutrements drew upon both the idea of diaspora and the institution of black studies. And he/they used them both to render the specific and localized concerns of black Canadians null and void. What is at issue, then, is how to theorize diaspora and account for its crucial transnational and outer-national political identifications, when those very practices can be used against specific black communities to render them powerless.[16] It might be that in thinking about the politics of diaspora and its ensuing offshoots — black studies and black cultural studies — that we have to address the question of imperialism. And that is a difficult thing to do in the context of identifiable groups who still remain inside/outside of their specific nations.

My readings of the Niagara Movement; Delany; Mary Ann Shadd; Gates's involvement in the *Showboat* debates; and the place of Canada in African-American crossings, then, are not intended to place the uninteresting question of black Canadian exclusion on the table, but to arrive via that circuitous route at two more important points. Of central concern to me here is the question: What might black studies not bear to hear? Or, what might black cultural studies allow us to hear? And in the name of what political project will that hearing be accomplished?[17] These questions sit at the centre of what I believe to be the cultural politics of theorizing black diaspora and the black Atlantic while avoiding the rancidness of new wine in old skins.

In more recent discussions, Wahneema Lubiano and Mae Henderson articulate what we might call a fear that black cultural studies has somehow usurped the space of black studies and in so doing has not recognized the importance of locating black cultural studies as the trajectory of black studies. Henderson in particular is concerned that "the emergent project of black cultural studies be situated in the context of Black Studies" (64). Undoubtedly, black studies mapped the terrain that has made present configurations of black cultural studies possible. As someone who came to black cultural studies via the routes of both black studies and cultural studies, I find their discussion both heartening, politically important, and unsettling.

Henderson's concern is that "black cultural studies threatens to re-marginalize a field of study [black studies] that became central during the Black Studies movement" (63). She writes: "I am less concerned about the displacement of African-American hegemony in black diasporic studies than I am by the erasure of a historical genealogy for black cultural studies that extends back for at least a century to the African-American critique of politics and culture formally inaugurated by W.E.B. DuBois in his landmark *Souls of Black Folk*, and later elaborated in his many studies, monographs, and autobiographies" (63). I agree with this genealogy, but differ with her on the issue of what is at stake in the move to black cultural studies.[18]

What is at stake, I believe, is the (im)possibility of Black Studies to live up to what Henderson identifies as its necessary reclamation "as a multidisciplinary, cross-cultural, and comparative model of study which places into juxtaposition the history, culture, and politics of blacks in the U.S., Caribbean, and Africa" (65). This vision of Black Studies is troubling because it does not attend to the cross-cutting constitution of black cultures and instead appeals to some geographic space of certainty. This is particularly the case when different permutations of all the mentioned groups exist with, and in, each other's locales. The dispersal of black people gestures to the limitation that Henderson places on Black Studies and might thus occasion the move away from it. Black Studies's continued dependence on ontology might not offer the room that black cultural studies offers for exploring difference, blackness as a sign and locus of ideas, and the contradiction and tensions of a diasporic connectedness, to name only a few.

If I might appropriate the metaphor of movement/motion, which I believe is crucial not only to diasporic principles but

also to black cultural studies, then what arises for me is the
appearance or desire for a particular stasis (there has been, if
I'm reading correctly, too much jogging going on). Now if
one ties this to the reception of British blacks in the American
academy a curious situation comes to the foreground. The
acceptance and celebration of the black British might be
understood in relation to an American desire to supplement
what they lack due to their abbreviated colonial past. Paul
Gilroy gestures to this when he writes: "[i]n these circum-
stances it is hard not to wonder how much of the recent
international enthusiasm for cultural studies is generated by
its profound associations with England and Englishness" (5).
Black British cultural studies, however, could not and cannot
escape its integral relation to the peoples of, and from, the
Caribbean (for example, C.L.R. James) and African-American
public intellectuals (for example, June Jordan). Questions of
creolization and hybridity find their way into the discourse of
black British cultural studies through the route of Caribbean
migration to England. What is interesting is the ways in
which Caribbean theorists, with a few exceptions, have gone
missing in contemporary black diasporic debates, and how
black Britain has become the privileged site of engagement.

I want to suggest that black Canadas are a matrix for the
contestations that are currently taking place in black diasporic
studies.[19] As a location for post-emancipation and post-
national independence for Caribbean migrants, and more
recently for continental African migrants, and as a sanctuary
for escaping enslaved African-Americans and their descendants, the multiplicities of blackness in Canada collide in
ways that are instructive for current diasporic theorizing.[20]
Furthermore, the official sanctioning of identity politics supported by the state, with a legislative multicultural policy,
places issues of difference and connectedness in a different

relation and configuration. Nation-state influence can (re)direct the potential political possibilities of meaningful diasporic conversations.

Black studies's (re)marginalization is occurring for many reasons, but chief among them is the various ways in which black particularities have been disavowed in many of the current discussions. Since the 1996 Olympics might still be fresh in our minds, the particularities of black difference and nation-state discourse(s) might appear clearer in a brief detour to that spectacle of nationalist frenzy. The disbelief of both white and black Americans that, not only did they not win the one hundred metres, but that their relay team was defeated by the black Canadian team, was more than evident.[21] The insistence by Michael Johnson and the American media that *he* is the fastest man in the world, despite that title usually going to the winner of the one hundred metre event, attenuates the limits of diasporic discourses. As Donovan Bailey recently stated, "[t]he claim is from Michael Johnson, and he's not even the fastest man in Texas..."[22] Now, this might appear trivial in the scheme of things, but it goes to the heart of what black studies might not bear to hear.

Bailey's comments gesture to his training in Texas and are just another example of the criss-crossing of black Canadians. Many fugitive slaves returned to the United States after emancipation (t)here and this practice has continued to mark black North American border-crossing. In the 1960s there were two types of crossings: one type was occasioned by conscientious objectors to the Vietnam war, while at the same time, some black Nova Scotians were leaving Canada and moving down the eastern seaboard after the razing of Africville.[23] That these crossings go missing in the discourses of black studies demonstrates how we cannot understand black studies outside of structures of imperialism. Black cultural studies, with its attention to locality in the context of globality, might be read as offering some space to explore the tensions of black studies.

Black Canadian identification with the incidents in Los Angeles in 1992, and the eruption of a small riot in Toronto, is yet another indication of transnational political identification that needs to be addressed. For example, the *dedordement* music of rapper Devon is a case in point. Repetition, reference, citation, circularity—all the characteristics of black diasporic cultures — are used by Devon in his sonic appeals for justice. Devon raps:

No, no, no, LAPD; ease up RCMP; ease up
Orange County; ease up
No OPP; ease up 52; ease up
Peel Region; ease up
Don't shoot the youth[.]

The intertextual and intermusical resonances of "Mr. Metro" ("And another one gone and another one gone/ And another one bites the dust") places blackness outside of national boundaries and requires us to theorize blackness as an interstitial space. Devon's signifying and testifying calls up a broader notion of blackness than state narratives would allow, for Devon refuses to reference only one nation in the sonic blackness he constructs. And while he does not lose a sense of locality and historicity, his political and artistic identifications exceed national boundaries.

The contested terrain of hip-hop is just one example which attests to the possibilities and the limits of diasporic theorizing. The insistence on reading rap and hip-hop only within nation-state parameters and an American context, has impeded and limited what kinds of discussions and what kinds of histories of hip-hop are possible.[24] This has consequences for the kinds of relations that are created and imagined by those of us involved in the production of knowledge in the university. Shifts from black studies to black cultural studies might be constituted through long and enduring dis-satisfactions with black studies.

It seems to me that discourses of diaspora require that black studies seriously considers diasporic exchanges, dialogues and differences. If I might use one more example by way of conclusion, a brief look at border-crossing on the part of another Canadian might shed some light on what I am trying to say. The release of Maestro Fresh-Wes's last album from New York raises a number of questions. Among those questions is Canada's difficulty with locating a black presence within. After two fairly successful albums (*Symphony in Effect* and *The Black Tie Affair*), Fresh-Wes argued that he had to leave Canada because the Canadian recording industry and other media, in particular radio, did not demonstrate support for rap artists. Fresh-Wes decided to run for the border, as the Taco Bell ads suggest (Taco Bell actually suggests a border that Delany favoured over the Canadian one — Latin and South America) and found himself in New York City. The album he released is titled *Naaah, Dis Kid Can't be from Canada?!!!* — and it clearly doubles and signifies in its naming.

The persistent refusal of mainstream Canadian airwaves to play rap music places musical blackness outside national narratives. Fresh-Wes's title both gestures to this, and targets the narrative of rap and hip-hop as an African-American invention. Through his title, Fresh-Wes suggests that the "dopest" rhymes can come from elsewhere, disturbing the foundations of the home of rap. At the same time, he worried geographic, cultural and national borders by releasing the album from the United States. He used his black Canadian alterity to disturb what appears to be a mimetic identification when he ran for the border packing his desires for hip-hop commercial success. Whether home is the nation-state, black studies, black cultural studies or all three, in the words of black Canadian poet Dionne Brand, "home is an uneasy place", and diasporic experiences attest to that unending restlessness.

"A Tough Geography"
Towards a Poetics of Black Space(s) in Canada[1]

We say that a national literature emerges when a community whose collective existence is called into question tries to put together the reasons for its existence (Glissant 104).

The word must be mastered. But such a mastery will be insignificant unless it is an integral part of a resolute collective act — a political act (Glissant 163).

So we're not going any place, and we're not melting or keeping quiet in Bathurst Subway or on Bathurst Street or on any other street we take over—Eglinton, Vaughan, Marlee. If our style bothers you, deal with it. That's just life happening, that's just us making our way home (Brand 80-81).

Walking Negro Creek Road

Settler colonies can be characterized by their struggles over race and space. Canada is no exception. The first phase of black demands on the Canadian nation-state must be considered in light of Africadian demands that land grants promised to them be honoured.[2] When some of those grants were indeed honoured, the quality of the land was suitable for little more than housing plots. This originary struggle over space, constituted through a specific and particularized Canadian racial discourse, is what we might call the racial geography of Canada.[3] National historical narratives render these racial geographies invisible, and many people continue to believe that any black presence in Canada is a recent and urban one spawned by black Caribbean, and now continental African, migration.

In 1967 Africville was finally and permanently razed. It continues to exist only in the memories of its former inhabitants and their descendants. Now, the desire to render black peoples and blackness an absented presence in Canada has been made literally and symbolically clear. More recently in Ontario, the offensively stupid claim of Holland Township Council, that using the word Negro in the 1990s was uncomfortable, led to that council changing the name of Negro Creek Road to Moggie Road. Renaming the road after George Moggie, a white settler, was yet another paragraph in the continuing and unfolding story of the ways in which Canadian state institutions and official narratives attempt to render blackness outside of those same narratives, and simultaneously attempt to contain blackness through discourses of Canadian benevolence. Thus blackness in Canada is situated on a continuum that runs from the invisible to the hyper-visible.

While contemporary poets, activists, oral documenters and archivists such as George Elliott Clarke, Delvina Bernard, Maxine Tynes, Syliva Hamilton (who is also a filmmaker), the singer/songwriter Faith Nolan and numerous others, have attempted to counter the writing of black people out of the Canadian nation, the process continues to unfold.[4] It appears that the collecting and documenting of evidence of a black presence that is underway in Nova Scotia is not occurring in

Ontario, Quebec, British Colombia and the other provinces. The importance of the Nova Scotian achievement is that it gives us the ability to create a language of blackness in Canada: one that is at once mindful of black migrant cultures, but also recognizes and acknowledges the true genealogy of black existence in Canada.[5]

Canada is a land troubled by questions of race and space, whether we are speaking of First Nations land claims, Quebec nationalism, or the "absented presence" of Canada's others. In 1993 the eruption of what was characterized as a "mini-riot" at a condominium complex on Dixon Road in Etobicoke, involving the Somali community, crystalized the issues of race and space in this nation. Accusations against Somali youths attempted to place their cultural practices firmly outside the nation, even when the accusations were ridiculous. A consequence of the "troubles" was that a move was made to criminalize Somali youth through the use of stringent enforcement of trespass laws. Somalis were made hyper-visible, in an effort to mark and to confine their movements and bodies in space and to a particular place. Nineteen ninety-three signalled the incorporation of the Somali community into the dominant discourses of race and blackness structured by North American white supremacy. That racialized discourse, fostered by and emanating out of slavery, is continually fashioned through an ideology that suggests that black bodies can and must be abused, misused, regulated, disciplined and over-policed. These practices of regulation and discipline occur in the effort to make belonging, as Dionne Brand puts it, "an uneasy place" (67).

Yet black people in North America continue to make both space and place theirs. This, however, is not accomplished by understanding their experiences as isolated and disconnected from other places and spaces. The political identifications of black peoples are crucial and essential to resistance. Making outer-national identifications with other black peoples is important to the kinds of struggles that might be waged within national boundaries. Dionne Brand, by working across different genres (poetry, short stories, oral history, historical and sociological essays, polemical writing, film-making and now the novel), has used her immigrant/citizen status to bring a new cartography to the question of race and space in the Canadian context. She redraws and remaps the Canadian urban landscape in order to announce and articulate a black presence that signals defiance, survival and renewal. Brand's work, located in the urban spaces of migrant existences, refigures the actual, literary and figurative landscapes of Canada, and so redraws boundaries of knowing, experience and belonging. But what is characteristically complex about Brand's work is that it offers no orthodoxies on blackness. Instead her Marxist, feminist, lesbian voice and political insights are the bases from which she articulates critiques of patriarchal and essentialist notions of blackness, as well as critiques of racism, patriarchy and class exploitation in Canada.

After The Nostalgia of Immigrant Writing

Nostalgia is dead. Dionne Brand's *In Another Place, Not Here*, a complexly woven tale of space, language, identity and place, is uncharacteristic in terms of recent (Caribbean?) black Canadian literature. Brand's refusal to construct a narrative of the easy nostalgia that has come to mark much immigrant writing is notable. *In Another Place* puts an end to, or at least signals the demise of such cultural representations and (literary) politics.

Comparatively, Cecil Foster's focus (in his two novels on the ways in which movement, or rather migration, to Canada has affected individuals) is still in large measure concerned with the politics of dislocation constituted via nostalgia for "home". It seems that one of the challenges facing contemporary black Canadian art is to move beyond the discourse of nostalgia for an elsewhere and toward addressing the politics of its present location. Foster's characters, in particular Suzanne in *Sleep On Beloved*, must deal with their inability to put home "behind" them. I am by no means suggesting that one's move to an elsewhere can only be made "successful" by jettisoning the past. Memory often will not allow that anyway. What I am trying to suggest is that "immigrant writing", and in this case "Caribbean (black) immigrant writing", is often shrouded in a nostalgic longing for a past that is neglectful of the politics of the present location. Interestingly, one might read Claire Harris's poetic collections, particularly her recent *Dipped in Shadows*, as another piece in the (re)ordering of black writers' concerns with the cultural politics of "home" — that is, Canada.

But in making these claims, Brand and Harris should be considered with another group of black Canadian writers who have made the question of space one of concern to their artistic endeavours.[6] George Elliott Clarke, Maxine Tynes, Carol Talbot and a number of others have continually emphasized place and space in their work — in particular the places and spaces which, for lack of a better term, I would designate "indigenous black Canadian space". This particular group of "indigenous black Canadians" have not garnered as much attention nationally as they should because their presence — the places and spaces they occupy — makes a lie of too many national myths (or raises too many questions) concerning the Canadian nation-state. Thus, in a perverse way, it is around Canadian blacks of Caribbean descent that definitions of blackness in Canada are clustered. The hyper-visibility of Caribbean blackness makes "indigenous black Canadians" invisible.

With Brand, I want to interrogate and speculate about what the category black Canadian might mean in the context of this historical moment. Brand's last three works concern themselves in no small detail with mapping a black Canadian poetics of space — "a tough geography" (40) as she puts it in *No Language is Neutral*. These efforts are important for the historians and sociologists who have not been able to furnish black Canada with a discourse that recognizes an almost five-hundred-year past, it is up to those of us engaged in other aspects of cultural work to articulate what that means. While I am in no way trying to position literature and its critics as the vanguard of cultural knowing, it appears to me that imaginative works often render much more complex and interesting constructions of our multiple historical experiences than other cultural forms. I think that in the case of black Canada this is particularly so.

George Elliott Clarke, in the important essay "A Primer of African-Canadian Literature", offers a genealogy of African-Canadian literature in which he makes some important claims concerning black writers in Canada. While Clarke is paying attention to the active and political deployment of a constellation of African-Canadian works in an attempt to combat "uninformed commentaries" (7) which reduce black Canadian literature to "West Indian Writers" (7), he also offers an interesting project for internal black dialogues, critiques and conversations. His essay suggests a paradigm for discussing not just black literatures in Canada, but also, I would argue, black cultures. Clarke suggests that "exiles and refugees" (7) are the primary source for black Canadian literature; he writes: "African-Canadian literature has been, from its origins, the work of political exiles and native dissidents" (7). This renders complex and fluid the very constitution of those who might and might not be defined as black Canadian.

Clarke's observation holds great promise for formulating a black Canadian discourse conscious of both the locality of national boundaries and the limitations of nation. It is in the context of exiles and refugees that I shall engage a discussion of Brand's *In Another Place*.

Exiles and Refugees

In Another Place, Not Here is the story of two migrant black women, Verlia and Elizete. Verlia's migration is legally accomplished; Elizete's migration is not sanctioned by state authorities. What these two women's stories allow us to see is the ways in which their existence redraws the boundaries of Toronto, Ontario and Canada. Those boundaries are redrawn in the way they resist brutality. Brand uses her characters' experiences to write a text that exists at/on the in-between space; in fact, the very language of the novel occupies the space of the in-between. Brand constructs sentences that bring Canada and Caribbean together in ways that remap both: for example, "She decided to get away from the mall and the Gladstone and began to walk the maze of streets trying to get to the sea" (56). Brand's seemingly strange sentences refigure Canada as we know it, implanting the experiences of black peoples, in this case black women, in the very crevices of the nation. Brand's accomplishment is what the black British cultural theorist Paul Gilroy calls "[c]ritical space/time cartography of the diaspora ... the dynamics of dispersal and local autonomy can be shown alongside the unforseen detours and circuits which mark the new journeys and new arrivals that, in turn, release new political and cultural possibilities" (86).

In Another Place makes demands upon space and place, and they're couched in the demarcations of an in-between. For black Canadians, living the in-between is conditioned by their inside/outside status in the nation-state; whether "indigenous black" or otherwise, in-between-ness in Canada is conditioned by a plethora of national narratives, from the idea of "two founding peoples", to multicultural policies, to immigration policies, to provincial and municipal policing practices, and so on. The impossibility of imagining blackness as Canadian is continually evident even as nation-state policies like multiculturalism seek to signal otherwise. The simultaneity of being here and not being here is, in effect, an in-between position. The prospect of in-between-ness is, however, not only produced by the state: it's also something black folks have chosen through their multiple diasporic and outernational political identifications. It is in both of the above senses that Elizete and Verlia make demands of the place(s) they find themselves in, whether they're Caribbean or Canadian. Elizete's flight from the Caribbean and Verlia's flight from Sudbury are not entirely differently conditioned: both exist in the in-between. Both women live an outernational existence characterized by migratory movement and particular political commitments and practices.

In *No Language is Neutral* Brand writes, "walk Bathurst Street until it come like home" (30), insisting and asserting a presence of blackness in Canada, or more bluntly, staking out territory. Her insistence is posed in the context of a national narrative which seeks to render her "the thin/mixture of just come don't exist" (29). The utterance of "just come" is one of the ways in which the life of the in-between is lived out. The idea of "just come" is crucial to the nation-state's construction both of black invisibility and hyper-visibility. Ludicrous excuses like discomfort with the word Negro are used to deny the evidence and existence of an early black historical presence which troubles and worries the national myth of "two founding peoples". Such practices make sense in the context of a sociological discourse of black anti-racism, emanating mainly from Toronto, which has constructed blackness in Canada in ways that ignore or pay only lip service to any black antecedent prior to the 1960s.

The discomfort of Holland Township's Reeve reveals the traces of the ways in which language has been used to denigrate and render black people less than human. Language is only one of the things that is at issue when folks who have been colonized talk back and resist. Remaking language, however, is the way to come to terms with the past in the present, as recent black post-colonial assertions insist. Thus those who marched on Negro Creek Road to retain its name were not just marching so that the visible and tangible evidence of the past would not disappear, they were also marching because reclaiming Negro is as important a part of black historical memory and experience as any other artifact or document.

Brand's use of language is essential to her re-ordering of Canadian literary realities because she brings new sounds and tonality to what may be considered Canadian. Her use of language signals the unsettled restlessness of the exile and refugee who must rechart, remap and regroup so that both self and collectivity are made evident and present. Black diasporic practices of language continually revise and reveal its constructedness, and also its importance in both domination and resistance. The potential of language, to disclose the discredited histories of black peoples, is evident in these practices of revision and reversal. In this sense, reclaiming and insisting upon the name Negro Creek Road is of immense importance. For it is the name, or what the language conveys, that denotes the history of black peoples in the province of Ontario.

Staking Out Territory

Dumbfounded I walk as if these sidewalks are a
place I'm visiting. Like a holy ghost I package the
smell of zinnias and lady of the night, I horde the taste
Ignoring
my own money thrown on the counter, the race
conscious landlords and their jim crow flats, oh yes!
here! the work nobody wants to do...it's good
work I'm not complaining! but they make it taste bad,
bitter like peas...
Our
nostalgia was a lie and the passage on the six hour
flight to ourselves is wide and like another world...
(*No Language is Neutral* 31-33)

If Negro Creek Road disappears from Ontario and thus
Canadian maps, memory and remembering will be the ghost
which haunts Holland Township and Canada. Canada's continued forgetfulness concerning slavery here, and the nation-
state's attempts to record only Canada's role as a place of
sanctuary for escaping African-Americans, is a part of the
story of absenting blackness from its history. Erasing all evidence of any other presence (First Nations and black) is crucial if the myth of two founding peoples is to hold the crum-
bling nation of Canada together in the face of Quebec's
impeding separation and declaration of nation status.

Many "negro creek roads" exist; they are yet to be found
and documented. It is particularly the symbolization of
"negro creek roads" that I want to explore because their existence announces the refiguration of the social, political and
cultural landscape of Canada. And it is not a barren one. If we
want to turn to recent history for a remapping of the

Canadian urban landscape, Toronto's Bathurst Street might best stand in as a ritualistic locus for migrant Caribbean peoples. The people who live in the in-between, neither here nor elsewhere, redraw and rechart the places/spaces that they occupy.

It is living in an in-between space that Brand, M. Nourbese Philip, Austin Clarke, Cecil Foster, Andrew Moodie and a host of other writers, thinkers, dramatists and choreographers articulate; in doing this they take a political and ethical stance which refuses the boundaries of national discourses. To be black and "at home" in Canada is to both belong and not belong. The Dream Warriors celebrate black diasporic connectedness and passion in their song "Ludi" by calling out and naming black home spaces in Canada and the Caribbean.[7] This naming is a practice of the in-between. For nation-centred discourse can only prohibit black folks from sharing "common feeling", especially when common actions seem to present themselves, time and again, in and across different spaces/places/nations.

In Brand's collection of essays *Bread Out of Stone*, "Bathurst" stands out as a statement about reconfigured space. When Brand reads the essay, its poetic qualities infuse a black diasporic orality into the polemic and "(re)tune" the sound of Canada. However, "Bathurst" is important for more than its tonal qualities. It chronicles the existence of the vibrant black, mainly Caribbean, community that existed on Bathurst Street in the 1970s. The essay is about space, time, culture and how black peoples' activism refashions Canada. Brand recharts urban identity and populates the literary sphere with black Canadians who recognize that "home is an uneasy place" (67).

"Bathurst" is important for a number of reasons, chief among them being the assertion and insertion of a black presence in Toronto, one that refuses to be silenced, to be made invisible and to exist solely on the margins of North American society. It is the refusal of marginalization in all of Brand's work that transfigures the space/place of domination. Bathurst is the space of self-assertion and political engagement that Verlia seeks:

> She finds a room in a house on a street off Bathurst. She chooses the street because of the barber shops on Bathurst. It is Sunday but she knows that on Monday this is where she will meet the sisters and brothers in the Movement. This is where she will cut her perm and this is where she will begin (155).

There is an ambivalence in Brand's (re)creation of Verlia's search for, and eventual discovery of, the Movement in Toronto. This ambivalence is the novelist's rendering, in her (re)telling, of the problems of nationalist discourse. It should not be overlooked that Verlia, who grows to become a feminist and lesbian, is always off — Brand does not put Verlia at the centre of nationalist movement. The reasons for this are obvious. Living in a room off Bathurst, where black male spaces — barber shops — dominate, means that Verlia's lived experience must be elsewhere. Brand is not creating a sentimental remembering of the Movement of the 1970s; instead she offers a reassessment of what might have been possible had all aspects of blackness been considered — especially questioning the masculinist tones of the Movement.

In this regard she ushers new tropes into Canadian literature. The importance of black and migrant urban space is revealed as Elizete evades immigration officers, changes names repeatedly to conceal an already invisible existence, and struggles to survive in the context of a hostile land.

Verlia, on the other hand, flees Sudbury because it's the site of black suffocation. In effect, the notions of exile and refugee status refigure contemporary Canada as a space where blacks do not belong. In addition, Brand's critique of patriarchal black nationalism brings black internal dialogues to the texture of Canadian cultures.

In Another Place is Brand's lyrical portrayal of the ways in which identity, place, belonging and the politics of self and collectivity are lived out and actualized in language. I want to focus on the remaking of the racialized, gendered and sexualized (literary) landscape of Canada, as another one of the important ways that Brand's novel disrupts Canadian literary practices. Moving beyond the discourse and literary tropes of "roughing it in the bush" and "survival" in a barren landscape (national tropes which deny a First Nations presence), Brand moves through an urban landscape populated with the usual suspects of Canadian migrant cultures. She brings to the Canadian literary landscape the bittersweet taste and metaphor of the tamarind—bittersweet because of its sensuality, its shape, and its hard core or pit.

Staking claim through naming is crucial to the project of redrawing the urban landscape of Canada. Brand names and traverses Toronto in an attempt to make it the "home" of Verlia and Elizete. In doing so she charts many of the home spaces of migrant Caribbean peoples in Canada. *In Another Place* is literally and symbolically a historical and contemporary map/guide to (black) Toronto. Bathurst, St. Clair Avenue, Vaughan Road, Christie, Bloor, Harbord, College Street, Oakwood, Danforth, Regent Park, Avenue Road, Yorkville, Yonge Street, these names exist alongside names of places and spaces in the Caribbean. The Gladstone Hotel, Van Dong Restaurant, Canadian National, factories, rooming houses, barber shops, parks and dance halls (The Paramount), are signifiers which locate place, names that refigure and claim, make one's presence felt. Through Verlia's and Elizete's eyes, voices and experiences we get a different and new cultural, political and economic map of Canada. Brand's recharting of the Canadian landscape is not in any way romantic. In *No Language is Neutral* she warns that "nostalgia is lie" (32) and in *In Another Place* Elizete's and Verlia's elsewhere, while remembered, is not romantically yearned for. The tales of activism that organize Verlia's life in the novel lead both to her feminist awakening and a critique of black patriarchal nationalism and heteronormative politics. Verlia demands more of black nationalism. Brand, in creating a character who not only challenges white supremacy but also calls into question and challenges the patriarchal and heteronormative politics of black nationalism, is surely redrawing the boundaries of blackness. In fact, she implodes those boundaries.

By mentioning Fanon in the novel, Brand acknowledges his important insight: that to understand black experiences only within the context of singularity (i.e. nation) is to render oneself continually vulnerable to the forces of oppression. Verlia and Elizete attempt to occupy the space between self and collective desires and expressions; this might be called a post-national black lesbian feminist space/place. When Verlia returns to the Caribbean — not in a romantic search for roots (no nostalgia is evident), but rather as an activist — she announces the possibility of change and makes demands on place and space. The latter is the imperative of black diasporic political identifications which seek both to refigure black experiences and to demand justice.

The Space of Pain

The space of pain is what gives teeth to the issues that
Brand confronts in *In Another Place*. By this I mean that
Brand's insistence on refusing to render the displacements
and reconciliations of mothers with daughters as simple and
uncomplicated is very important.[8]

> These women, our mothers, a whole generation of them,
> left us. They went to England or America or Canada or
> some big city as fast as their wit could get them there
> because they were women and all they had to live on was
> wit since nobody considered them whole people (230).

Pain is often the trace that binds women together in Brand's
work, but in the novel pain is also the necessary evil that must
be worked through if reconciliation of any sort is possible.
Indeed, she maps a number of pains that occupy the unspoken
spaces of blackness in Canada:

> They sent for us, sent for us their daughters, then washed
> our faces in their self-hatred. Self-hatred they had learned
> from the white people whose toilets they had cleaned,
> whose asses they had wiped, whose kitchens they had
> scrubbed, whose hatred they had swallowed... they saw
> their hands swollen with water, muscular with lifting and
> pulling, they saw their souls assaulted and irrecoverable,
> wounded from insult and the sheer nastiness of white
> words... They made us pay for what they had suffered...
> They did not feel redeemed by it but they themselves had
> been so twisted from walking in shame that they twisted
> our bodies to suit their stride (231).

While Brand as novelist must rethink the context and contours of racist Canada, she also unsentimentally conveys the wretched impact of racism as it is played out in mother/daughter relations. Echoes of Jamaica Kincaid's rendering of daughters' relationships with mothers are evident in her work. The estrangement of daughters from mothers, as Brand writes it, sits at the heart of the question of community, and parallels the question of black nationalist rhetoric and its failures to fully address black multiplicity.

(Re)newals

The *Globe and Mail's* Joan Thomas suggests that Brand is too angry even when she is at her best. Thomas's back-handed praise of Brand is the kind of stuff of which black erasures in Canadian culture are made. The comparison of Brand's work with Toni Morrison's is simultaneously accurate and troubling, especially when Brand is criticized for not having Morrison's "largeness of spirit" (C20). Fallaciously inferring that there is no anger in Morrison's work denies the ways in which the redemptive and transfigurative moments in her texts are arrived at. What seems behind these readings is a tendency to read black women writers within what we might call "the mammy tradition" — black women, this school of criticism implies, should make all things right or at least smooth everything over.

To arrive at the moment of transfiguration, or to even open up its possibility, the space of anger in black diasporic culture must be explored by black artists, critics and others. And it's just as important for us to question the idea that anger has no place in literature. Thomas' comment, that "memory is full of the sour taste of tamarinds" (C20), is her call for Brand as novelist, and black people generally, to forget a past and present of pain. In recognizing that memory has forgetting as its twin, Brand writes of "the skill of forgetfulness" (13) as something that's learned in the context of the dismissal of women, but important for recognizing how the concerns of those resisting are also dismissed and denied.

Long-time readers of Brand's work have seen her continually redraw and remap the oppressive landscapes of Canada. In short stories like "Blossom, Priestess of Oya, Goddess of winds, storms and waterfalls", "At the Lisbon Plate" and more specifically "Train to Montreal" (all from *Sans Souci and Other Stories*), Brand began the project of rewriting the racialized space of Canada. *In Another Place, Not Here* is a tour de force which recharts this project.

The authorities who sanction the racialized space and place of Canada will continue to have to face and come to terms with the exiles and refugees in their midst. The struggle of diasporic blacks for space in Canada has a long genealogy, and a trajectory that will continue to cause reverberations across all aspects of the national body. I invoke the body, or rather, bodies, here because what is ultimately at stake is the space and place that bodies, both actual and symbolic, occupy in the nation's imagination. Black Canadian literature's unruly bodies will continue to insist upon a space where justice and freedom are possible, and, as Brand puts it, "it doesn't matter that it's Toronto or a country named Canada. Right now that is incidental, and this city and this country will have to fit themselves into her dream" (159).

The Politics of Third Cinema in Canada
Reading the Narrative of Clement Virgo's *Rude*

Discussions concerning the black body have gone MIA in public debate. While debates in cultural studies rage around black cultural productions, attention to the black body, or rather, black *bodies*, has been minimal. I want to shift our gaze back to the black body and the ways in which Canadian Clement Virgo's first feature film *Rude* maps it as a site for the writing of a contradictory *socio-religio narrative* of pain, threat and desire. The black body in Western discourse is a marked body, marked with the history of enslavement and disenfranchisement. Or to draw on an Ellisonian metaphor, the black body is both invisible and hyper-visible. Simultaneously, black bodies are unruly, resistant, and the sites of various renewals. Black bodies are engaged in a per-formative struggle to produce their own markings.

My use of the body here follows the way Michel Foucault's delineations of the term understand that discourses of medi-cine have intervened in the historical production of particular and specific modes of thinking and talking about the body and sex. Foucault's micro-histories demonstrate how the dis-courses of medicine have generated an operational schema of discipline and regulation, and this clearly has implications for thinking through representations of black bodies in various sites. Bodies as machines, docile bodies, bodies as controlled by others — these paradigms are just a sample of the ways in which slavery operationalized and marked black bodies as a blank canvas to be written on and inscribed with the desires of the master. As David Goldberg puts it:

> the rise of the racist expression and its accompanying violence of material deprivation was rendered *theoretically* possible only by a change in paradigm from the seventeenth century onward for viewing human subjects. The new philosophical assumption that bodies are but machines, opened the way to some extreme novel development in technologies of physical power and bodily discipline. These technologies of discipline and power were superimposed upon human subjects; they encouraged docility by reducing even *social* subjectivities, or at least some forms of social subjectivity, to physical dimensions and correlates (53; emphasis in the original).

Slavery has had an enormous unacknowledged impact on how we might think about bodies in the West. The operationalization of power on bodies to mark, discipline, and control can be understood as enacted through the very enslavement of bodies. Thus the discourse(s) and realities of slavery have come to mark how we see and think about bodies, especially black bodies, and blackness. The actual evidence of the breeder and the stud in slavery stands out as an example of the forms of domination, regulation, and discipline of the body as machine.

Ideas which tie black bodies to nature, labour and savagery pervade our imagistic landscapes.[1] How do these images/representations relate to the enslavement of black bodies? How have black bodies resisted, reversed and undermined the discourses that attempt to mark their bodies? How have black people produced their own discourses about their bodies? What are the various ways in which black people mark their bodies as sites for the expression of joy, pleasure, pain, lack and desire? In terms of cultural production, black people have offered various meditations on these questions, and they're crucial for moving beyond the moment that Stuart Hall has called "the end of the innocence of the black subject or the end of the innocent notion of an essential black subject" (32).

Third Cinema in Canada?

Third cinema has been one of the places where an exploration of the end of black innocence has taken place, but evidence of third cinema in Canada is slim. Characterized by its political savvy, a poetics of critical, leftist theory and aesthetics, and its ability to unsentimentally challenge political and cultural orthodoxies of all kinds, third cinema has really not emerged in the Canadian cinematic scene.[2] Thus the third cinema that I am referring to emanates mainly out of Britain (in particular black Britain); various parts of the formerly colonized world, for example the Caribbean and Africa; and in independent films from the U.S.A. Third cinema is characterized by the works of filmmakers like the Sankofa Collective, Black Audio and Film Collective, Isaac Julien, John Akomfrah, Reece Auguiste, Avril Johnson (England), Ousmane Sembene, Felix de Rooy, Haile Germina, Charles Burnett, Zienbu Davis, Julie Dash and Euzhan Palcy to name only a few. The work of these filmmakers, from the late 1970s to the mid-1980s, challenged the ways in which we have come to understand and imagistically represent black communities.

Recently two feature films directed and written by black

Canadians signalled the possibility of a late-blooming third cinema in Canada. Despite some ten to fifteen years of third cinema, these two black Canadian entries have both failed in terms of content, narrative and aesthetics, to be as politically conscious as their black British and "third world" counterparts. The celebrations that have followed the release of Clement Virgo's *Rude* and Stephen Williams's *Soul Survivor* have failed to adequately address their truncated politics.[3] The films might be set in Canada, but one might want to ask: What makes them black Canadian films?

Some of the central tenets of third cinema can be located in the ability of filmmakers like Isaac Julien, John Akomfrah and Julie Dash to recast debates concerning place, space, history and belonging into the very crevices of their films in order to disrupt normative notions of nation and belonging. This has produced interesting and new aesthetic features in the work of third cinema filmmakers, ones that speak to complex manifestations of communities in the making. Thus third cinema did not merely announce itself by claiming to be the black representative, but rather it questioned and brought a criticality to the very practice of naming/representing — as an incitement to/for critical dialogue and conversation.

Clement Virgo's *Rude* is aesthetically playful and populated with a host of features meant to signal the "blackness of blackness". Music probably plays the most obvious role in the attempt to bring a black aesthetic pitch to *Rude*. Reggae and gospel stand out as framing devices which play "speaking" roles in the film, punctuating speechless characters' actions. In fact, it's music — reggae and gospel and sometimes rock — that might be generously read as the film's creolizing or hybrid base. The three musics act as a surface upon which is written various kinds of distress, yet the way they are specifically used in particular scenes unravels any attempt at reading them as truly creolizing forces. For example, gospel is often the background music accompanying the scenes in which Maxcine (Rachael Crawford), a character who has had an abortion, appears. In the end, the socio-religious use of music often tends to act as a moralizing force.

The place of home, a site that is usually complicated by the hybrid practices of third cinema, is not at all in question in *Rude*. The film is set in one of Toronto's urban ghettos; and while stylized shots of the cityline are etched into the filmic text, place is clearly not an issue. The narration by the pirate DJ Rude (Sharon Lewis) makes statements like "the land of the Zulu Nation and the Mohawk nation meet... while the rest of Babylon gets to ponder its immigration policy" and suggests that issues of place might be important, but this is never explored in any sustained manner. Instead, the insidious discourse of heritage makes a clear demarcation circumventing the archipelagic migrant cultures of the Caribbean in Toronto to produce a direct link and lineage to a Jamaican heritage and a film populated with derivatives of African-American culture. The inability to work with the imagined realities of blackness in Canada are clearly not broached by the filmmaker.

In spite of: The Realism of *Rude*

To merely signal *Rude* as the typical hood film would not do justice to the director's pyrotechnical talents. Virgo plays skillfully with both a nonlinear narrative and assorted camera shots, angles and double takes — whether it is a character repeatedly falling down, running but not advancing across the screen, or an action repeated twice — his talent for aestheticizing film is undeniable. The aesthetic practice employed is mainly one of repetition, and this, of course, is a fundamental element of black diasporic cultural practice: one which can be seen in any number of black cultural representational strategies. Despite these strategies, *Rude* cannot evade its influences. Both the film's narrative practices and the story that takes centre stage are structured by the usual suspects of the hood film genre: the police, familial breakdown or tension, jail, drugs and criminal activity. Manthia Diawara, outlining some of the elements of the hood film or what he has called "the new black realism", identifies rites of passage, moments of crisis, black male responsibility for community, the existent violent realities of black urban living, characters who change with the unfolding story line and characters who move to a "higher understanding" of the world as fundamental to the genre. These elements, while in some broad sense being concerned with the black body, do not and cannot account for the need to critically assess various forms of black resistance where black people insist on marking their bodies as more than masculinized victims.

Rude is steeped in the hood film genre. Issues of crime, familial dysfunction, and violence pervade the imagined world of the film as the central issue becomes the (re)gaining of black manhood for General (Dean Witt). The narrative of *Rude* consists of three tales which are kept together by the lubricating vocal twists of a female pirate DJ named Rude. Here Virgo's narrative choice echoes Isaac Julien's *Young Soul Rebels*, which makes important use of pirate radio DJs, and Spike Lee's *Do The Right Thing*, which constitutes the community through radio.

The fundamental difference between Julien's and Virgo's use of pirate radio is the fluidity of the way in which Julien's pirate DJs move across place, space and time. Rude, the DJ in Virgo's narrative, is stationary — she moves neither metaphorically nor literally — and this limitation is in itself a small example of the ways in which Virgo's narrative creates a static conception of blackness. In *Rude*, three stories unfold over an Easter weekend: each consciously gestures to issues of life, death and resurrection. In fact, these issues propel the three narrative tales of the film. I would point out, however, that the overburdened socio-religious narrative structure of *Rude* fails to produce a politically transfigurative moment.

***

Discourses concerning blackness have clearly shifted since the 1950s and the turbulent 60s and 70s. The collapse of grand narratives of black nationalism in the 60s and 70s paved the way for black postmodern practices, articulations/utterances and aesthetics. For me, black postmodernity is an unsentimental approach to addressing the complex and varied histories of diasporic black peoples. A quick comparison of the television sitcom *Good Times* (1970s) and *In Living Color* (1980s/90s) bares this point out. Both shows attempted to represent something called blackness but the former was cast in a particular mould to represent and validate blackness and thus black people as legitimate in the context of Euro-American politics and culture. On the other hand, *In Living Color*'s irreverence toward all aspects of American culture presented and parodied various "sacred" American cultural texts, both black and white, in a conscious effort to unwrite any notion of a homogenized American/black subject. It is this kind of unsentimentality about blackness which will allow us to focus on the actual politics of bodily production and engagement.

Political actions are doubly important when resorting to a homogenized black subject becomes merely another fiction to which some black subjects refuse to acsribe. Thus we see, in the three narratives of *Rude*, an overlapping narrative construction which produces a homogenized black subject obsessed with the properties of producing and explicating a "correct" black masculinity.

Tale 1

General returns home, after spending time in jail, to a wife who is a police officer; he is unemployed and literally has no money, but must put up with increasing demands from a growing son who wants various kinds of commodities (running shoes, ice cream, etc.) General's dilemma is essentially moral: should he return to the drug trade so that he can be a father and "real" man to his son. General's self-image clearly depends on his ability to provide financially for his son; failure to do so makes him a "failure" and threatens to strip him of his manhood. His dilemma is resolved by his refusal to return to the drug trade, but this decision leads to a confrontation between him and Yankee (the white drug lord), and his wife has to shoot Yankee to protect General and their son.

This narrative partakes heavily in the conventions of the hood film and it follows the kind of realist narrative that has become the fiction through which black (male?) urban life is now conceived. Such narratives invent, centre and stereotype black masculinity, arguing that it has become impaired or flawed because it lacks the necessary resources to produce "good patriarchs". The repetition of these narratives has come to occupy a sacred place in contemporary black popular culture, foreclosing the possibility for much more interesting imaginative works.

Tale 2

Maxcine is a woman in distress, dumped by a boyfriend, Andre (Andrew Moodie), who disapproves of her decision to abort an unwanted pregnancy. She hardly speaks in the film.

The camera pans to shots of Maxcine's aborted love child, returned as a ghost, at about the age of six or seven, dancing while Maxcine tries to renegotiate the terms of her new single life and the evidence of her past life with Andre. Maxcine's life is communicated to viewers via both an answering machine and the emotional outbursts that result in her smashing the tools of her trade (the mannequins she uses as a window dresser). By the end of the film Maxcine has apparently seen her love child walk away from her, and this suggests that she has somehow come to terms both with the abortion and the end of her relationship with Andre.

Virgo's direction and camera work are quite smart in this narrative. Not only does he cite and play with current debates about technology and hardware as sites for exploring identity, but he gives it back to the audience in a haunting, cinematic language. It is also through this narrative that he is able to cite other black diasporic cultural workers and theorists in his film. In particular, we can note the intertextual conversations between Toni Morrison's *Beloved*, where a dead daughter returns from the grave to help her mother come to terms with the past. But even more immediate to cinematic concerns is the citing and riffing off of Julie Dash's *Daughters of the Dust* a film in which the narrative is revealed to the audience through the voice of an unborn female. Virgo's cinematic virtuosity is clearly playful, and sometimes reveals a diasporic sensibility.

Tale 3

Jordan (Richard Chevolleau) is a boxer who is emotionally tormented because he's participated in a gay bashing (called a "lynching" in the film). Jordan must deal with his own homoerotic tendencies, and as the film unfolds he begins the process of both coming to terms and coming out. He is finally liberated when the man he helped beat up retaliates, slapping Jordan in the face several times. It's a scene which demonstrates the filmmaker's artistry. This incident takes place with Jordan sitting on the same bench the "marked" gay man used to cruise from. Jordan must endure this "beating" as both repentance and resurrection. The over-earnest attempt to link black heterosexism and homophobia to a black past of white racial terror by using the word lynching, however, makes this narrative too simple and contrite.

Bodies are at stake in all three tales: bodies in trouble. Yet the narratives, cast in a socio-religious mode, are unable to adequately demonstrate the trouble that these bodies are actually in. Instead, they become the canvas upon which a moral tale of love and loss is inscribed.

The Queer Body of *Rude*?

The three tales are not only tied together by *Rude*'s verbal commands (which direct viewers to look out for particular actions), but they are also linked by the exploration of masculinity. I want to focus here mainly on the last tale (of my narrative) because the filmmaker has pinpointed this story as the tale which will teach the audience something. Clement Virgo has said:

What I saw and heard in black music: a lot of homophobia in the music and a lot of homophobia in the culture. I wanted to talk about this; I wanted to write a character that had this duality. When we think of young black men, we think that they are the ultimate symbols of machismo, of masculinity. I wanted to explore the idea of a young black man who is strong and a boxer, but the duality is that he is also gay" (20).[4]

Any effort to unravel the numerous assumptions behind Virgo's attempt to bring a critical discussion of sexuality to black Canadian cinematic representations is mangled by these comments. The black/queer body is asked to stand in as the site upon which the inscription of violent heteronormative desires are lived out. The filmmaker, however, is not able to be pedagogical about the ethical relations of race, sexuality and community in a way that does not necessarily produce a victim. This particular writing of the black body sits counter to the ways in which third cinema's best work has inscribed bodies in cinematic texts.

In Julien's *Young Soul Rebels* the centrality of queer bodies to the ethicality of community is not only marked by the imagined and real violence of gay bashing, but also, in a much more radical way, by a love scene questioning not only heteronormative positions concerning sexuality but also positions on questions of border-crossing racial lines (a black man and white man make love).[5] Julien's political incitement means that he does not shy away from the difficult politics of representation. It also means that he is clear about the importance of critical encounters in terms of the ways in which images are used to make a political case. His work, then, is about the "unleashing of unpopular things"[6] as a way to engage in dialogue and conversation concerning important issues. It is this difficult knowledge that the representation of the queer bodies in *Rude* does not accomplish.

***

Central to the narratives of both *Young Soul Rebels* and *Rude* are music and musical cultures, and by extension the cultural practices of black youth are implicated. More specifically, hip-hop culture has come to mark some of the contestation that surrounds how we might understand any discussion of black bodies. The counter-poetics of hip-hop cuts across a number of political positions: they range from radical to nationalist and espouse conservative and progressive political positions. These cultural practices are representative of a moment characterized by the withering of post-emancipation/post civil rights narratives of liberation. Thus some of the importance of black postmodernity rests in the complex and torturous terrain of recognizing the contradictory moments of black youth cultures. Virgo's assertion, that the motive for a tale about homophobia was conditioned by the homophobia in the music and culture, is simultaneously both hopeful and a trap. It is a trap because it fails to acknowledge black difference or name, in specific terms, where, when, and how this homophobia is articulated. Engagement in the politics of representation means that writers/directors take responsibility for their work and words. To critique a generalized black culture is no longer enough.

Culturally, black youth have demonstrated a real concern with the body and its performance. Their use of the body echoes the various ways in which black cultural practices have always treated bodies as a canvas upon which historical and contemporary social relations may be signified, inscribed and rewritten. The body, therefore, is not only used as a biological mechanism, it also works as a site for the contestation of social relations as those relations relate to acts and actions of power on and through the body. In Kingston, Jamaica, some gay men refer to themselves as "sports", naming themselves as different in the context of a culture that can sometimes be hyper-masculine and punishingly heteronormative. The sporting body of the boxer in *Rude* could be read through a gaze which fixes that body in relation to the popularized heteronormative and hyper-masculine narratives of black male youth. But to do this through boxing and a masculine assertion of self in violence is a refusal to see the scope of queer sensibilities. This might be the fundamental difference between Virgo's *Rude* and the work of someone like Isaac Julien.

In the essay "Bodies and their Plots", Hayden White offers a reading of the history of writing the body — or rather histories of writing bodies — via Freud's essay "Instincts and their Vicissitudes". In White's complementary re-reading of Freud he demonstrates how certain bodies are asked to inhabit specific histories. *Rude*'s narrative asks the queer body to inhabit only the place of victim. One can say that such a tale is well known and easy to tap into. Why not ask the queer body to inhabit the site of pleasure, of joy, or the site that constitutes the only "normal" position in the film? By having Jordan engage in a gay-bashing incident before he begins to come to terms with his homoerotic desires is to inscribe upon the queer body the very hatred that the writer/director hopes to dismantle with the tale. Hayden White puts it this way:

> Or, a drive may be disengaged from its original object of gratification and turned back onto its subject, so that what started out as, say, hatred of another ends up being expressed as hatred of oneself. This produces the masochistic body, the body that consists of little more than the sum-total of pain it has inflicted upon itself (230).

Furthermore, White states:

> The history of the body — or, indeed, the history of bodies and, beyond that, the histories of bodies — presumes the possibility of identifying a normal body, in which or

on which changes and transformations can be traced across different parameters of time and space. Moreover, a history — any history, any kind of history — in order to locate and identify the body whose "story" it would tell, must postulate if only implicitly some kind of anti-body, an anomalous or pseudo-body. This anti-body marks the limit or horizon that the normative body, in the process of its development, evolution, or change may not cross without ceasing to be a body proper and falling or degenerating into a condition of bodilessness (232).

What is at stake in *Rude* are bodies and their histories or bodies in history. In many cases those histories are mangled by a socio-religious narrative which gestures towards a moralizing conservative politic. This might appear to be a harsh criticism for a film with a "gay" plot. What this postmodern moment of lost innocence can be pedagogic about are the various ways in which heteronormative positions can be postulated. The "story" or "plot" does not, in and of itself, guarantee a transfigurative moment.

Because bodies, actual and imagined, are at stake, it is imperative that we make representations matter beyond the discourse of merely seeing ourselves. Representational strategies have to account for something, and the politicality of any given representation can never be read as innocent or apolitical. Thus across the three tales of Virgo's *Rude* a number of images come together which speak to the troubling, lopsided politics of the film. In one scene Yankee is portrayed as a devious and sinister drug baron who is willing to inject potentially HIV-tainted blood into a desperate, down-and-out drug addict. When this scene is read alongside the tale of Maxcine's distress and the bashing that Jordan, in his denial of self, both participates in and is a victim of, the moralizing tones of *Rude* betray the imposture of a radical politics because the writer/director fails to see how these images and narrative representations leak into each other.

If reading bodies can be pedagogical about anything today, the reality of HIV/AIDS and the various ways in which it cross-cuts communities has to be taken into account in our political commentary on the body. That the film *Rude* cannot produce a conscious narrative about the rhizomatic nature of how bodies relate and even collide in space is unfortunate because the fact is unprotected sex can result in an unwanted pregnancy and abortion: and this needs to be addressed. Similarly, the realities of drug use and unsafe sexual practices, combined with the ways in which queer communities have been politically active in terms of HIV/AIDS and the real consequences the virus has for bodies, needs to be accounted for. The film's structure does not allow for the possibility of its tales cross-cutting (characters from one tale do not show up in another). The writer/director did not envision an audience whose reading practices might just bring them together. This is tragic because, as we know, and as the film itself partially demonstrates through the sinister exchange of blood from one character to another, bodies leak into each other. They are not merely the separate entities that we think them to be — discrete and infinitely individual — bodies connect and come together at various moments, and the resultant leaks can have dire consequences. Narratives, as well, leak into each other: and narratives also have consequences. Thus if Virgo really imagines his audience to be homophobic ["Because I assume the audience is homophobic and I have to take them along to the point where they discover that I love this character who's gay and they have to say to themselves 'hmmm, wait a minute, I've got to think about this'" (20)] as he has said, then what he fails to acknowledge is that readers do not have to read or experience his narratives as separate.

And in this war of representation that surrounds the politics of HIV/AIDS, even when intravenous drugs are a part of the story, the underlying subtext remains one of a queer culpability. Virgo's rescue mission of a gay subject in his film is unwritten by the leaks or traces of one narrative tale to another. There must be another way to teach folks about love.

***

Postmodern blackness can be articulated as having its lineage in the discourse and movement histories of emancipation, civil rights, black cultural nationalism and the technological and industrial re-organization of the post-World War II capitalist world. These moments have been characterized by the emergence of a strong and large black middle class (in America and in some parts of the third world) since 1970, and the decline into stricter confines of poverty for black working classes. Simultaneously, feminism and gay liberation have disrupted any easy assumption concerning black community and sameness. The tensions inherent in the mimetic and alteric faculties in black communities have not been clearer; and these are the beginnings of the elements necessary for what I call black postmodernity. The relations between history and the body remain clear. It is in black urban areas that bodies are consumed by drugs, high rates of infant mortality, AIDS, and early violent deaths. It is both those same places, and the bodies which inhabit them, that provide the basis for much black cultural production today. It is those bodies that are at stake in what we do, when we do it, as folks engaged in the project of cultural work — whether you're a filmmaker or critic. So, in the final analysis, art necessarily speaks for some kind of politics. *Rude,* locked within a socio-religious narrative steeped in the politics of conversion, however, fails to register the kind of politics of transfiguration that allows folks to think what they have not before thought: when they encounter Virgo's cinematic representations they're not incited to trouble the body.

"Keep on Movin'"
Rap, Black Atlantic Identities and the Problem of Nation

History is always written from the sedentary point of view
and in the name of a unitary State apparatus, at least a
possible one, even when the topic is nomads. What is
lacking is a Nomadology, the opposite of a history.
(Deleuze and Guattari 23) [1]

Collecting Dispersals

Soul II Soul's signature song, "Keep on Movin'", asks its
listeners to "keep on movin' don't stop". It's an injunction on
stasis and an invitation to accept the fluidity of identity and
cultural practices as an ever-present and upfront part of how
we might understand the self and the world. The album, in
both its idea and its organization, is representative of this fluidity. Jazzie B, the musical arranger, vocalist, rapper and
founder of the ensemble Soul II Soul, for example, acts as the
only reoccurring member. Jazzie B, or the "Funky Dread", is
himself a hybrid of a British roots culture, characterized by its
syncretic mixture of Jamaican Rastafarian stylings and
African-American popular cultural practices — all of which

are elements refashioned and shaped to fit the specificities of black Britain's music and dance scenes. Soul II Soul's music is a journey through contemporary forms of diasporic black music (popular culture) and so Soul II Soul symbolically and actually represents the fluidity of black diasporic relations and cultural expressions and exchanges.

The emergence of the ensemble on the international music scene in 1989 signalled what might be characterised as the undeniable cultural exchanges and expressions that exist between diasporic black cultures. The announcement of those relations was made in both song/sound and image. The cultural references, while positioned in the specific and local of black Britain, referenced and cited the "deeper structures" of diasporic black cultures. Soul II Soul released three more albums, all of them international successes: these releases blend a number of black musical genres — rap, dance music, rhythm and blues, soul, reggae and jazz. As well, the creative founder of Soul II Soul, Jazzie B, has become involved with the Jamaican music industry and collaborated with a number of other artists.

In this sense, Jazzie B aided in contemporary refigurations of the Middle Passage, a site which continues to represent one of the primary psychic spaces that black people (both dispersed and continental) need to continually address. The trauma of the Middle Passage is a cultural silence that only now is slowly being recognized as a constituent part of black diasporic memory. Langston Hughes lovingly reimagined Africa for "new world" blacks with negroes dreaming of the Nile; Zora Neal Hurston, in *Moses Man of the Mountain*, rewrote the Exodus story, opening a space for discussions of leadership and community to take centre stage in relation to remembrance and possible futures; and the desire to reconnect with Africa has been expressed by works like Frantz

Fanon's *Wretched of the Earth* and *Towards the African Revolution*, M. Nourbese Philip's *Looking for Livingstone*, Toni Morrison's *Beloved*, Charles Johnson's *Middle Passage* and Edward Kamau Brathwaite's *Middle Passages* — all of which attempt to make the "unspeakable spoken" and thus place the "discredited" and "subjugated" knowledges of the "dark diaspora" on the agenda of contemporary politics by reconfiguring the history/memory of the Middle Passage for black Atlantic people.[2] These "literatures of reconnection"[3] represent a significant change in how we might understand both the social and cultural formation of black diasporic communities and what those communities might share beyond phenotype.

What I want to do is look at the ways in which the citational and referential practices of rap music disrupt the notion of the modernist nation-state. The referencing and citing of other songs/sounds or musicians in rap is not the only gesture towards a larger community. That rap musicians persist in making links between practices and events in their localities to practices and events beyond the boundaries of their locale is important in terms of demonstrating how various state authorities are understood as seeking to control blackness both locally and extralocally. For example, the occurrence of narratives concerning relations with police exist in numerous rap songs from various places. The practices of citing and referencing across borders, when coupled with the movement of actual black bodies across state lines proves disruptive, in profound and disturbing ways, to the romantic, fictive narratives of the unified nation-state. This is particularly true when the songs seem to suggest that similar practices (for example, the regulatory and disciplinary practices of police and immigration officers) are used to control blackness in different locales. The transmigration of the racial metaphor that "black equals criminal" seems to work across space and time, and suggests that while locality is important, some practices spill their borders. It is this spillage that is recouped as a moment of diasporic black identification.

Evidence of the collapse of the unified nation-state is everywhere today. Glaring examples exist in the former Yugoslavia, the conflicts in Somalia and Rwanda, and the resolution of conflicts in Ethiopia and Eritrea. Even the recent peace treaties between Israel, Jordan and the Palestinians seem to suggest the emergence of a new Palestine — though it's not necessarily a "nation" in the modernist sense. In fact, the creation of an Israeli nation-state in 1947 could be read as a signal of the collapse of the modernist nation-state, even before the fall of the Berlin Wall. Israeli citizenship, for example, was not dependent upon the "usual" criteria of birth and so forth. "Jewishness" — which is much more malleable than birth right or language — was more important to the organization of the "new" Jewish/Israeli nation-state. What constitutes Jewishness, however, has been questioned. Some felt that the Ethiopian Falashas, for example, might only be tangentially Jewish, and that their religious practices might be too anachronistic. Russian emigres, who often have only one Jewish parent, have also posed problems. Recent reports of a group of people from the Indian sub-continent claiming Jewishness and seeking membership in the nation-state of Israel have also pushed the limits of Israel and called into question the very notion that the nation-state is founded on sameness.[4]

The histories, memories and experiences of dispersed peoples always act as a transgression of nation-state principles. If we look at the history of Canada, with its ethnic mix of English, French, Ukrainians, Italians, Jews, Germans, Poles, Portuguese and other Europeans, as well as Japanese, Caribbean, Chinese, South Asian, continental African, black

Canadian and Native peoples, what we get is a complex picture of who and what the Canadian might be. All of these groups (except for the Natives) migrated at different points in time, and have found themselves placed differently in the narratives of the nation, in ways which complicate the fiction that the modern nation-state is constituted from a "natural" sameness. While it is clear that many of the European groups have been able, through the mechanisms of white supremacy, to become Canadian in ways that those who are not white have not been able to achieve, it is also clear that each successive migrant group represented a rupture in the myth of the nation as constituted from sameness. What the European groups demonstrate, as well, is that sameness is constituted in the process of forgetfulness, coercion and various forms of privilege and subordination.

It is, however, the migration of non-whites that has continually disrupted the fictions of the nation-state because they show up attempts to both conceal and deny otherness within the nation and to produce racial sameness as the basis of the nation-state. Canadian fictions of sameness seek to make acceptable the massacre and continued disenfranchisement of Native groups and the continued oppression and resistance of formerly colonized people who have migrated to the "satellite" nations (Canada, America, Australia, New Zealand, etc.) of former colonial powers. It is these Others who have most clearly challenged the fictions of nation-state sameness as a racialized code that produces Canada as a "white nation". Consequently, the Somali refugee community in Canada has also aided in the continued transgression of nation-state fictions of unity and oneness. The emerging Somali community might represent the newest black migration to Canada, but as a whole they are quickly having to become "black" in ways that other black Canadians can identify with. What does rap music have to do with Somali refugees, and the construction of the Canadian nation-state? It is this question that has provoked what follows.

Theorizing the Nation-State

Theorists of the nation-state have continually debated the terms that make the state intelligible to those who identify as members or citizens. Benedict Anderson[5] pinpoints "print-capitalism" and its unification of language patterns and use as constituting the ways in which the nation-state became imaginable for large groups of people who shared a common language. Anderson locates three reasons for how the nation became an imagined community based upon print-capitalism. First, the printed languages became "unified fields" which allowed the literate to communicate exclusively with each other and thereby create an imagined community of readers. Second, the printed language gave the vernacular languages a new fixity that produced codes and usages that only those who read could relate with. Third, these new standard languages created enclaves of power that benefited those who knew the codes and could thus decipher and trade in discussions concerning important questions of the day.

Anderson's schema is important for understanding how a nation might imagine itself in the moments of early state formation, and it's particularly salient for European nation-state formation. But his schema becomes much more murky when applied to nation-states founded after colonial encounters. For these places the politics of language use and its relation to state formation is often played out between the twin forces of internal strife and, more importantly, local class antagonism and neo-colonial or imperialistic practices (for example, countries where the official language is English but the everyday language is different. In Malta, English is the language of business but Maltese is the language of everyday use). Post-colonial nation-states raise a number of important questions and necessitate reconsiderations of Anderson's theory, and perhaps most important among them is the need to refigure the role that language plays in a national consciousness. On the other hand, Anderson's[6] theory does help us to understand the ways in which the "Janus-faced" nature of the nation is achieved (Bhabha).[7]

The Janus-faced nature of the nation is its often two-sided, contradictory, conflictual and unclear articulation of what it means to be a citizen. Official multicultural policy in Canada plays such a role. The policy textually inscribes those who are not French or English as Canadians, and yet at the same time it works to textually render a continued understanding of those people as from elsewhere and thus as tangential to the nation-state. It also characterizes those others as people whose static cultural practice are located both in a past and elsewhere. Bhabha's Janus-face metaphor alerts us to the fact that the nation-state is always about more than at first seems apparent. Conceiving the nation in this way helps us to understand the textual practices of the nation-state as they work both to subordinate and produce inside/outside binaries, and also suggest other possible positions for cultural subjectivity.

In a more recent elaboration and contemplation on the theory and politics of the nation-state, Partha Chatterjee[8], has both supported Benedict Anderson and critiqued him. What is important about Chatterjee's argument is his insistence on the need to develop a language of nation-state theory and politics that can seriously account for community. Using India as his case study he argues that the models for nationalism were so determined by Euro-American notions of the state that the possibilities for post-coloniality were severely limited. Chatterjee suggests that such limitations have led to a separation of public/private notions of community which results in a normalization of the state as an ostensibly public entity. Chatterjee writes:

> The result is that autonomous forms of imagination of the community were, and continue to be, overwhelmed and swamped by the history of the postcolonial state. Here lies the root of our postcolonial misery: not in our inability to think out new forms of the modern community but in our surrender to the old forms of the modern state. If the nation is an imagined community and if nations must also take the form of states, then our theoretical language must allow us to talk about community and state at the same time. I do not think our present theoretical language allows this (11).

Chatterjee poses a fundamental question, one that forces us to confront whether building a community is possible. In the context of Canada, the nation as imagined community is organised around the idea that it's innately based upon phenotype and language. Thus the Canadian nation-state has no way of making sense of communities founded across and upon difference. Official multicultural policy in Canada actually works to produce a definition of community that's about one's relationship to another nation-state. Because community is understood as the public qualities of language, "culture", and ethnicity, official multicultural policies at both the federal and provincial level support this idea through a discourse of heritage — in Canada "heritage" always means *having hailed from somewhere else*. What follows will demonstrate, through a number of readings of black Atlantic cultural practices, that an understanding of how community might be constituted outside the discourses of the modernist nation-state can be derived from diasporic cultures.

Narrating the Multicultural Nation

The "textual accomplishment"[9] of Canadian multicultural policy has been the main focus for addressing the ways in which the Other is imagined or not imagined in the Canadian nation-state. The multicultural narrative is constituted through a positioning of white Anglophone and Francophone Canadians as the founding peoples of the nation, with a "special" reference to Native Canadians.[10] All Others exist and constitute the Canadian ethnic mix or multicultural character. Thus the colonizing English and French are textually left intact as "real" Canadians while legislation is needed to imagine other folks as Canadian.

In everyday and common-sense usage, *multicultural* means that all those who are not white (i.e., of European descent) represent the ethnic mix. The debates concerning Neil Bissoondath's *Selling Illusions*[11] are an indication of this. His arguments are mainly constructed around dismissing the claims that people of colour make concerning various forms of domination in Canada. And all of the debates and discussions which took place in the mainstream media about his book were centred around the cultural practices of those who are not phenotypically white. The use of multicultural as a category of naming and administration, however, closes down as many possibilities as it opens up because it can also be used to reference the "white ethnics" (Italian, Portuguese, Polish, Yugoslavian, etc.) who are often invoked on "special" occasions to demonstrate the economic promise Canada offers new immigrants. (One recent example occurred on a news segment called "On The Street"; it showcased the "success" of a former Yugoslavian who now owns his own Pizza Pizza franchise after only fourteen years in Canada, [*CBC Evening News with Bill Cameron*, 1994]). Primarily though, multicultural, as a category, is reserved for those who need to be imagined as adjunct to the nation. And they are usually people who are not "white".

The other important issue that needs to be identified here is the way in which Canadian state multiculturalism locates specific cultural practices in an elsewhere that appears to be static. The various arts funding bodies — the Canada Council, Ontario Arts Council, Toronto Arts Council — not to mention theatre groups, artist-run spaces, museums, and galleries, all continually produce the fiction of Canada as a place of whiteness.[12] Thus the key word "heritage" organizes the approach that the state takes towards the culture of the other. Some might like to argue that it is multiculturalism that is the main narrative structure of the intelligibility of the Canadian nation-state, but often such arguments do not take into account the important ways in which popular notions of multiculturalism as meaning "non-white" are replayed in state narratives. So while the specific narrative of federal policy does not define multicultural as "non-white", discussions of the questions of immigration and education, for example, often tend to engage in the popular notion of multiculturalism as referring to "non-whites". These appropriations of the term are rife with the recurring myth of Canada as a benevolent, caring and tolerant country that adapts to "strangers" so that strangers do not have to adapt to it.

Canadian rap artists and dub poets (who are now being referred to as "spoken word artists") have continually challenged both the notion of benevolence and belonging and how these notions are constructed by and through the dominant discourses of the administrative categories of the nation-state. They have referenced and alluded to official forms of multiculturalism as textual attempts to hide the inequities of Canadian society. As well, they are at the forefront of challenging the various fictions of what Canada is, and their work is an attempt to produce new fictions of what Canada might be.

The Leaky Category of Black

Clifton Joseph[13] is one of Canada's leading dub poets. In his poem/song "Pimps" he ridicules not only state sponsored multiculturalism, but in a double-voicing, signifying[14] mode, he also locates those who are named by the media and government officials as community leaders as "pimps". They are the people who, he says, pedal-push the discourse and language of race relations "to get some money position or their kicks". What Joseph attempts to address in his poem/song is the relative complicity that those who are willing to be marked and marketed as representatives of "ethnic" communities find themselves in. Those inside/outside positions allow for proscribed access to the practices and discourses of dominant authorities. For Joseph these individuals are "multicultural pimps". On the album that features "Pimps" the relations of "diasporic identifications" are made clear and evident.

The hybrid jazz-funk of his song/poem "Chant for Monk 3", remembers Thelonius Monk through chant and song. Using his voice as both instrument and instrumentation for the lyrics, Joseph brings Monk back to life in what can be identified as repetitions of black cultural practices which continually reproduce the circularity of black cultural expression.[15] It is Joseph's repetitions that signal his disruption of the Canadian nation-state as we know it — for by not only chanting for Monk, but by engaging in the uncanny and intangible practices of black diasporic cultures, Joseph locates his sense of self beyond the boundaries of the nation-state. It is those musical transgressions that continually recur to disrupt the romance of the unified nation-state. Joseph's work unravels and makes it necessary to (re)contain blackness or attempt to render blackness absent from the nation. However, as Morrison[16] has argued about the American situation, blackness remains an absented/presence in the imagined community and landscape of Canada, and continues to work as a foil to whiteness. Blackness represents what Canada is not, and thus Joseph's identification with other black people, across space and time, resists the notion of the specificity of the nation-state as offering an unique experience or history. At the same time, his identification with other blacks insists on more from the Canadian nation-state.

Like Joseph, Lillian Allen has also positioned an "elsewhere"[17] that is both a reference to and a citation of the history of black diasporic experiences in her poems/songs. These histories often diverge from the concepts and the practices of the modern nation-state. Allen[18] sings/reads on the track "I Fight Back":

ITT ALCAN KASIER
Canadian Imperial Bank of Commerce
these are privilege names in my country
but I am illegal here
...
I came to Canada
found the doors of opportunity
well guarded
...
And constantly they ask
"Oh beautiful tropical beach
with coconut tree and rum
why did you leave there
why on earth did you come"

AND I SAY:
For the same reasons
your mothers came[.]

Allen dismantles the notion that the nation-state is familial and protective. But even more important for my purposes is her construction of the nation-state as "something" that must be fled. Clearly, Allen (rather the poem's narrator) had to leave an "elsewhere" to find herself in Canada. The migratory practices of the dispersed are plainly charted, and both colonialism and neo-colonialism are invoked in the process. From Allen's perspective post-coloniality simply does not deliver all the goods. Also just as important (for my purpose here as well) are the ways in which she deconstructs, or at least makes available the resources needed to deconstruct, the myth of Canada as a benevolent, caring and tolerant nation. She is "illegal here", and those who imagine themselves "Canadian" position her as an outsider when they ask "why on earth did you come"? Allen's deconstruction is not some mere acquiescence to "outsiderism", however: she "fights back", calling up the history of European colonial expansion and even more recent European migratory crossings ("For the same reasons/your mothers came"). Her poem, in fact, might be read as a reinvention of universality from the underside.

What Allen, Joseph, Dionne Brand, and rappers like Devon, Maestro Fresh-Wes and the Dream Warriors (whose work I will discuss later) suggest about black migratory politics/histories and experiences is a continual (re)negotiation and (re)articulation of what nation, home and family mean. All these artists produce work that can only be accurately described as ambivalent and ambiguous in its relation to the nation-state. They at once want to hold on to it (nation), as both something that is Canadian and a product of "elsewhere", and to reconstruct it as something much greater than the western modernist project of nation-building suggests.[19] Such practices often leave them embracing what can only be characterized as a diasporic understanding of "nation", one that's constituted through history, experience, and positionality. The more problematic versions of this are expressed as a romantic, pastoral, pre-colonial Africa of kings and queens and overdetermined notions of gender equality. Such versions are founded on what Wole Soyinka refers to as a "saline consciousness"[20] because of the geographic centredness of the narrative. In a world where black diasporic experiences seem to converge and diverge in important ways, these artists force us to continually rethink and reassess what we mean by nation, home, and community.

Devon, who is the best and clearest link between dub poetry and rap music in Canada, and who toured with Lillian Allen and Clifton Joseph before moving more firmly into popular music, is also much more symbolically fluid in his work. It is evident that a "nomadic aesthetic" informs the work he has produced to date. I want to focus on one of his songs that continually engages in the citational and referential practices that I have suggested organize black diasporic cultural practices because it gives texture to the arguments that I am making here. On his first album, *It's My Nature*,[21] Devon, like Soul II Soul, works with a large body of black musical genres — though rap and funk are central. The track "Mr. Metro" illustrates the ways in which black diasporic identifications work. The song was first released as a single in 1989, and it served as an emotional call for an end to police violence against young blacks. It is the police and/or those who enforce "law and order" (i.e., Immigration officers, security guards, teachers, etc.) that continually recur as the principle "administrators" through which we might continue to speak of diasporic political identifications that exceed the boundaries of the local. What those narratives often reference is how similar "actors" seem to be involved in the regulation and discipline of black bodies — even across national boundaries.

Police relations tend to be one of the most pressing issues for many diasporic black communities. Whether we are talking about the Rodney King incident, or police shootings in Canada, Jamaica, Barbados, or Britain, the police seem to be the agents through whom the dominant culture enforces its position. Devon, whose band is called (in signifying tones) the Metro Squad (a play on the Metropolitan Toronto Police force), in "Mr. Metro" raps:

> Metro's number one problem
> Is that no one really trust them
> Causing all this tension
> For something I wouldn't even mention
> Pick up *The Star*, pick up *The Sun*
> Headline "Metro gets another one"
> And another one gone and another one gone
> And another one bites the dust.

His lyrics locate one of the many policing practices which situate blackness outside the nation as criminal, deviant other. At the same time, these policies also work to contain blackness within the nation; because, the argument follows, black bodies must be managed, policed and controlled.

Arguments and policies that position black youth as pathologically criminal, that say strict action is needed to curtail deviant behaviour — for example, the Scarborough school board's "Zero Tolerance" initiative against school violence — evoke long-held beliefs about black people as criminals. Those policies suggest that black people need to be managed with a firm and strict hand. Zero Tolerance policies draw on historical practices of slavery that position the black body as uncivil: the social integration of the black body is possible only if it's firmly managed, policed, and, from time to time, not-so gently reminded of who exactly is in charge. Devon's music aims to resist and rework narratives that, across time and space, seek to subjugate black bodies. His contribution to an album from which proceeds supported voter registration and education in the recent South African elections is just another example of diasporic ethics at work: community is clearly built across the boundaries between nations.

For the Love of "Nomadicism"

It is the subjugation of black bodies that is most evident in the ongoing debate around community and thus nation that is occurring around the situation of 3,000 Somalis living in one of Canada's condominium complexes. Dixon Road, in Etobicoke, Ontario, is home to about 3,000 of Canada's 70,000 Somali refugee claimants.[22] The district is also a conservative, white, middle-age, middle-class suburban neighbourhood, built in the 1970s when suburbia offered an escape from what was perceived as the too-quickly-growing city infused with its flux of immigrant workers and increasing crime. The area around Dixon Road was promoted as a place to raise a family on a stable middle-class salary and instill what could now be called good family values. This was the case until the 1980s, when the Somalis arrived.

By the summer of 1993, the "problem" had firmly announced itself with a "mini-riot" in the parking lot of the Dixon Road condominium complex. One of the "riots" was sparked when security guards issued a parking ticket to a Somali resident on July 30, 1993. Since then, the area has been a hotbed of controversy, singling out all those who Lillian Allen[23] names in her poem/song as: "Immigrant, lawbreaker, illegal, minimum wager/refugee". The white residents attempt to argue that the problems come from an "elsewhere", and this defines the Somali community as outside what is allowably and imaginably Canadian.

In 1992 the then Conservative Minister for Immigration refused to increase the quotas for Somali claimants wanting to come to Canada. He argued that they were "nomadic" and would not settle down. He was not using the term critically like Deleuze and Guattari[24] but as an anthropologic putdown rife with ethnocentric clutter. Because of this prejudice, he could see no sense in increasing the number of Somali entry visas. They would only stay for a short period before they would roam off somewhere else. Following the federal immigration minister's comments, the provincial Liberal Party made it its policy to "expose" Somalis who were either "unfairly" collecting social assistance or engaged in some practice that might be construed as contravening their refugee status.[25] Reports concerning everything from social assistance cheques being used to fund the war in Somalia, to illegal herbal practices, to genital mutilation or female circumcision (naming is important here depending upon one's stance on the issue) made headlines in the Canadian press. Folks somewhere were working overtime to make sure that Somalis never became a part of the imagined community and landscape of Canada.

While the reports attempted to place Somalis outside the Canadian imaginary, at the same time they were also concerned with how to manage blackness. Describing the Somalis as nomadic was an attempt to make them culturally unintelligible just as they were being forced into the North American black criminal paradigm. The desire to regulate and discipline blackness was exposed when condominium owners hired security guards to patrol and contain *The Somalis* (blackness). The "nomadicism" of blackness has caused a great amount of concern for the keepers of Canadian national identity — a Canadian identity that can hardly come to terms with its slave holding past, let alone deal with the contemporary existence of black bodies in their midst.

The first few Somalis arrived in Etobicoke in 1989 — the year Soul II Soul emerged internationally, commanding us to "keep on movin' don't stop", and the year that Devon released "Mr. Metro", his plea to police to "ease up, Don't shoot the youth". They chose Dixon Road because it was near the airport, never imagining that such a choice would be used to position them as outsiders. Theirs was not a choice of privilege but one of pragmatic necessity. Living on Dixon Road made it easy to meet migrating relatives and friends at little expense (taxi fares); as well, the area provided relatively cheap housing. This is how the decisions of the world's migratory peoples are made: the need for cheap housing is the primary reason behind the "blackening"[26] of the Somali population in Ontario.

By blackening I mean to signal two important but related ideas. First, that nation-state administrators try to force what it means to be black on people through various mechanisms of domination and subordination. They are, in effect, telling you that you have very little, if any, relation to the nation. This process often involves arguing that black people are primitive, backwards, and not worthy of citizenship. Contemporary modifications of these myths are much more complex, and they're constantly shifting in late capitalist North America, where blackness is also a commodity (i.e., like hip-hop cultural artifacts, music and clothing). On the other hand, blackening also signals the various inscriptions that black people mark their bodies with (t-shirts, jewellery, etc.) and the discourses and articulations that both contest and resist subordination and domination. The articulations of lifestyles that do not continually respond to a reflex of domination is important to this process. Blackening as a performance, then, is how, at any given point in time any particular person marked as black might act out a discourse of blackness from the multiple positions that are possible. This acting out, whether as subordination, resistance, or something else, can often be forced. It depends upon the situation one finds one's self in. However, blackness is also a way of being and becoming in the world. Blackening, then, is the continual fluidity of the process.

To white condominiums owners, the everyday practices of the Somali community (especially their food odours and gatherings) were an affront to "Canadian ways of living". As Homi Bhabha writes: "The scraps, patches, and rags of daily life must be repeatedly turned into the signs of a national culture, while the very act of the narrative performance interpolates a growing circle of national subjects"[27]. It is these everyday differences, that refuse the subordinating discourses of the nation, which have led to what can only be characterised as the fascist imposition of condominium statutes of exact and minute detail upon the Dixon Road housing complex. Complaints about food odours, and cultural differences that some residents just can not understand, not to mention ludicrous accusations about everything from feces in elevators to apartment overcrowding, have surfaced in attempts to position Somali residents as unsuitable. For Somalis the "scraps, patches, and rags of daily life" are not being recouped as a sign of national belonging and culture; instead, they are being used to position them as outsiders. The absentee landlords that the Somalis rent from have been virtually silent about the alleged abuses that the condo owners have enforced with hired mock police (security guards). They simply collect the rent to pay their mortgages and/or make profits. So how does the Somali community under siege in Etobicoke relate to rap music and black Atlantic cultures?

The condominium statutes are being enforced to the letter by a security guard service patrolling the complex. What the guards actually do is police the Somali community. They've in effect been hired to enforce statutes designed to address accusations of Somali parking violations, vandalism and so on. Thus the guard service is representative of the macro-political practice of policing black bodies at the micro-level. On the regional and national, or macro-level, the various metropolitan police forces manage 'blackness', while on the micro-level security guards with dogs do the trick.[28] Ultimately, it's the stringent policing of the Somali community that has led to the two specific incidents that the local press has labelled the Dixon Road "riots". Policing practices have clearly conditioned and fostered the recurring debates about the place/space of blackness in the Canadian imagination.

When Devon raps:

> No, no, no, no, LAPD; ease up RCMP; ease up
> Orange County; ease up
> No OPP; ease up 52; ease up
> Peel Region, ease up Don't shoot the youth.
> ("Mr. Metro")

he is signalling that the management of black bodies by various police forces organize a transnational blackness. While Devon's song is located in the specific and the particular of various Canadian localities, his metahistorical commentary suggests that approaches to blackness are somehow related across time and space. Thus Devon's invocation of Orange County and the LAPD are not mere examples of naming but of naming with a point in mind, one that demonstrates the articulation of a border-crossing sensibility. His is a practice that strikes at the epistemological foundations of how black bodies are perceived and treated within the confines of the nation-state. Furthermore, his practice is one that reconfigures the nation-state by making links which produce more rich and textured histories/memories of black positionalities across space, time and nation.

Devon's rapped plea of "Don't shoot the youth" resonates and reverberates loudly, especially when one considers that in the case of the Somalis it is the youth who have resisted and who are the ones being marked as trouble-makers in a "troubled community".[29] The processes of criminalization are underway. Trespass notices prevent youths from visiting friends in other buildings. Blackness has taken on a whole new meaning for Somalis, and this has led one community leader to remark that their troubles are "an education for their children, preparing them to lead the lives of *blacks* in a white land" (emphasis added).[30] The performativity of the category black here suggests that Somalis who probably did not expect to live with the North American discourse of race intervening in their daily existence, have to do so now — simply in order to survive.

"Keep On Movin'"

In the summer of 1994, when Canada's financially successful rapper Maestro Fresh-Wes released his new album from New York, his "new home", his intentions were clear. The CD was titled *Naaah This Kid Can't Be From Canada* with the "Can't" underlined for emphasis. Fresh-Wes makes a signifying move that opens up a number of ways that we might think about a trans-national or diasporic blackness. First, his insistence that the "kid can't be from Canada" is a disruption of the idea that the "dopest" rap songs can only be performed by African-Americans. Fresh-Wes takes a shot at ethnic absolutist notions which attempt to historicize rap as an African-American invention and thus write black Atlantic exchanges out of rap's historical narratives. As well, he made it clear that his relationship to Canada was at best ambivalent (and possibly non-existent) — he left the nation. On the other hand, "naaah this kid can't be from Canada" could be Fresh-Wes' response to the discourses of nation that continually position his black body outside of Canada. Geneva Smitherman[31] argues that the role of double negatives is important in black speech patterns as an indication of the affirmative, thus Fresh-Wes' "Naaah" and "Can't" represent an assertion of national identity: in this way he worries the category Canadian.

The location of his new home is also important. Because while it might represent his desire to be marketed by the forces of American capital that could expose him globally in ways that Canadian capital cannot, he's located in a city of nomads, and, in particular, black migrant peoples. His movement symbolically suggests that black allegiances to "nation" are contingent upon the ethical practices of state administrators and narratives of the nation. This is neither a nomadic politics of play nor an example of the anthropological, colonialist idea of the exotic nomad, wandering and wild; but rather a disruption, contemplatively so, of the modernist nation-state. "Home is not where the heart is": it's where the self might be differently desired, imagined, lived and experienced.

Fresh-Wes' flight south reconfigures yet another myth of Canada's racial past. Yes, slaves from the U.S. fled north to Canada, "land of the free". But Canada's racial forgetfulness *has* resulted in a Canadian articulation of blackness that can sometimes seek, and desire to work with, a form of racism that speaks its name differently in the south (the form of American racism that does not mask itself as benevolent). Ironically the work of Canadian literary critic Frank Davey[32], which announces the "post-national" state, still locates the discussion of nation within the confines of Canada's modernist growing pains — it's the kind of two solitudes analysis (the English/French dualities and tensions) that does not begin to get at the ways in which the work of Other Canadians, some of whom he reads, creates too much dissonance for talk of nation to be heard.

As I suggested earlier, diasporic cultures can teach us much about the demise (or at the least the troubling of the category) of the nation-state. Like Davey, Canada's well-known postmodern theorist Linda Hutcheon[33], in an attempt to demonstrate how Other Canadians ironically split the image of what is Canadian, creates a number of readings that do not allow for the ways in which the Others of the Canadian imaginary find themselves both inside and outside the nation. Hutcheon reads the work of Dionne Brand, for instance, alongside Italian poets, positioning all of them as producers of homogenized ironic "immigrant" works that split the category Canadian. Yet one is left with no sense of how the histories of those who seem not to be able to live out or perform the discourses of whiteness are differently incorporated into the nation and thus possess divergent "immigrant" histories. Even progressive critics like Davey and Hutcheon, those who are willing to announce the collapse of the modernist nation as we know it, seem unable to read in complex and engaging ways the histories of those whom Gilroy[34] has termed the "counterculture of modernity", or who I call the "pre-postmodern postmodern voyagers".

The contemporary politics of race and nation in Canada, to echo M.G. Vasanji, represents "no new land". However, the promise remains: "the fighting back" of the Somalis and rap artists alike might reconfigure, remap and chart a notion of nation as a new land not concerned with narratives of geographic and textual boundaries but a nation that is constituted through the practices of justice, ethical politics and progressive race relations.

"No Language is Neutral"
The Politics of Performativity in
M. Nourbese Philip's and Dionne Brand's Poetry

The work has no hereditary soil. It is nomadic. Writing cannot forget the misfortune from which its necessity springs; nor can it count on tacit, rich, and fostering "evidences" that can provide for an agrarian speaker his intimacy with a mother tongue. Writing begins with exodus (Michel de Certeau 319).[1]

For the word has the potency to revive and make us free, it has the power to blind, imprison and destroy...The essence of the word is its ambivalence, and in fiction it is never so effective and revealing as when it mirrors both good and bad, as when it blows both hot and cold in the same breath. Thus it is unfortunate for the Negro that the most powerful formulations of modern American fictional words have been slanted against him that when he approaches for a glimpse of himself he discovers an image drained of humanity (Ralph Ellison 24-25).[2]

English
is my mother tongue.
A mother tongue is not
not a foreign lan lan lan
language
l/anguish
anguish
-a foreign anguish
(M. Nourbese Philip 56). [3]

I remember then, and
it's hard to remember waiting so long to live... anyway
it's fiction what I remember, only mornings took a long
time to come, I became more secretive, language
seemed to split in two, one branch fell silent, the
other
argued hotly for going home
(Dionne Brand 31).[4]

"Tongues Untied"

Understanding exodus as central to the writing of the black
diaspora might be one way of addressing the shifts, disjunc-
tures, displacements and interruptions of writing (in) the
diaspora. In writing the black diaspora, exodus is performed
as an incitement to dialogue because the writing concerns
itself with mimesis and alterity. The tensions of the copy or
sameness, and difference or otherness, are mapped into diasporic works as the very basis of their logic. I specifically use
M. Nourbese Philip's *She Tries Her Tongue Her Language
Softly Breaks* and Dionne Brand's *No Language is Neutral* to
address the performativity of black diasporic writing and
speech acts because they utter a politics of difference that
open up new kinds of possibilities.

These possibilities are made evident by the contingent meanings in both texts, an engagement with questions of *verbing*[5] and an articulation of what is meant by performance and performativity. Philip's and Brand's (re)writings are part of a black feminist diasporic remapping of sexist and racist accusations launched against black peoples' language and speech: accusations which suggest that black language and speech are inarticulate, that blacks lack the ability and capacity for artistic expression.[6] Words are the surgical tools that Ellison says bleed blackness of its humanity. Yet both Philip and Brand use the ambivalence of words to announce personhood and utter new possibilities.

As well, both Philip and Brand move beyond the reclamation of language to push Ellison's insight, that "fictional words have been slanted against him (sic) that when he approaches for a glimpse of himself he discovers an image drained of humanity" (25), to its limits. Since Philip and Brand are cognizant of the slant Ellison describes, they construct new sites for locating the self and making meaning in the world. Writing from in-between spaces, they manoeuvre across territory that places them on the frontiers of "postcolonial" and "postmodern" expressivity. Their poetry flows between the interstices of mimesis and alterity. Their actions constitute a redrawing of the image of self, and they offer a new gaze that is a second look because they drag along the traces of a historical past, which makes why a second look is necessary and even possible obvious. Theirs is no mere rewriting; it's a challenge to continually foster the grounds for a possibility of the new.

Black Language and Performativity

Drama, theatre and film studies have long held particular traditions and notions of performance, performativity and performer as crucial elements of how "identity" is understood in relationship to a question of role(s). Only recently, however, has the discourse(s) of performance moved beyond theatre, drama and film studies in a concerted effort to address not only the "fabrication" of the role of the actor, but to think through the very politics of staging within the confines of role playing. Role playing and its relationship to other roles (social, cultural and economic) has taken on a renewed and contested nature. Performance might be understood as that which Mae Gwendolyn Henderson, when writing about Toni Morrison, argues is a practice that "historicizes fiction and fictionalizes history" (64). Moving beyond notions of acting and role playing in drama studies, performance and performativity have become crucial to thinking through the politics of language practices as representations of complex identifications. As critical engagements with African-Caribbean/Canadian women writers continue to emerge, the performative structures of their language play becomes an increasingly important area for those attempting to understand their interventions and (re)constructions.[7]

Black people in the Americas have had an immediate relationship to identity and identification as twin acts which constitute performativity. This stems from the ways in which slavery produced spaces for particular forms of identity, identifications and disidentifications. Being forced to perform for the master in a number of different ways meant that a relationship to identity for diasporic black people manifested itself as something that could be invented, revised and discarded when no longer useful.[8] We might think about identity as a performance or acting out which puts into operation, or responds to, a set of discourses that have been a conscious and unconscious part of black diasporic cultures. Without being exhaustive, these un/conscious gestures can be looked at in terms of black peoples' use of language and their (re)writing of English, Spanish, Dutch, French and Portuguese; their (re)appropriation of derogatory performances like minstrelsy; the importance of the photograph and cinema;[9] the (re)invention of musical sound; and a plethora of other act(ion)s that make clear a notion of fashioning and invention of the self.

It is this (re)invention of the self that makes the study of performance, performativity, and their relationship to both structures of identity and practices of identification, important avenues for thinking through the mimetic and alteric structures of feeling among black diasporic people.

Musical cultures have long characterized black peoples' relations to basic notions of performance. In 1963, LeRoi Jones (now Amiri Baraka) published *Blues People: The Negro Experience in White America and The Music that Developed From It*, in which he outlined and historized the development of blues and jazz as only possible within the crucible of an idea/experiment called America. In particular, the chapter "Swing: From Verb to Noun" (142-165) attempts to demonstrate how jazz was appropriated from black people and made into a white musical form with rigid rules — that is, jazz became a formulaic genre. Baraka attempts to explain the stasis of jazz by arguing that it, like the blues, moved from verb (that is doing) to noun (that is stasis). His argument here is very important because the fluidity of music, its susceptibility to change, is crucial for its political potential. Jazz as noun cannot possibily alter America; as a verb, possibilities exist.

In a more recent essay, Nataniel Mackey, while paying homage to Jones, signifies[10] (in this instance an inversion) on him and titles his essay "Other: From Noun to Verb". Mackey is intent on demonstrating the performativity of black language and he argues that a continued verbing as resistance is practiced by engaged diasporic poets and musicians who continually (re)write and (re)invent form(s). I rehearse these partial retellings because inside of them lies a trace from which we might quite usefully think through the politics of performance and performativity in relation to black cultural production. More specifically, the study of black performativity impacts on how we might understand and at least engage with blackness as something that is continually provisional and an act of doing — verbing. It is in the continuity of verbing (doing) wherein the "possibility of possibilities" lies.

I believe that Philip's and Brand's poetic works continue the verbing of language, and in the process, of blackness. Andrew Parker and Eve Kosofsky Sedgwick write:

> But if a spatialized, postmodernist performative analysis like the present one can demonstrate any one thing, surely it is how contingent and how radically heterogeneous, as well as how contestable, must be the relations between any subject and any utterance (14).

They suggest the contingency of meaning as it moves across different spheres. To access that contingency and glean some of its meaning, it has to be understood that the performativity of various utterances cannot and do not guarantee the revelation of any one historicity (Butler 12-13). What performative utterances offer are the traces of various references, citations and repetitions that constitute "dramatic and contingent constructions of meaning" (Butler 136). But if these contingent meanings hold any importance to this project, it is in how they allow us to better address questions of community and freedom; or rather, questions of politicality. Philip's and Brand's poetic works perform the fluid movement between "hegemonic and ambiguously hegemonic discourse"[11] to utter black feminist and lesbian words which write/construct new black and white histories.[12]

Performativity in this project is meant to signal, and thus put into "public" space, crucial questions concerning both the limits and excesses of community. Because freedom is tied to the structures of community, whether "real" or "imagined", is an important consideration here. As Wilson Harris argued in an essay that was a response to the *fatwa* placed on Salman Rushdie:

> A love of Justice born of a voyage in space cannot be real until it gains cross-cultural resonance within a theatre of the creature where the ceremony of politics may perceive its obsessions undercut and transformed: a ceremony that so enacts, and re-enacts itself, that it *sees* within and through its own *blind* one-track logic and circumscription of history... (11; emphasis in original).

Harris posits that notions of community as sacred[13] have become the grounds upon which freedom is impinged, and it is only through "cross-cultural resonance(s)" that any hope might be possible at the twilight of the twentieth century. Philip's and Brand's language desecrates communities in an effort to (re)build ethical and just places that might be called home. The recognition and highlighting of the act, the performance, *the verbing of being*, becomes increasingly the element that must be addressed. I say *must* at the expense of appearing rigid, because it signals my desire for acting/actions.

This project, then, performs one tiny aspect of black cultural studies. My text acknowledges the possibility of working with difference not as the substance that must be dissolved but as the very thing that needs to be engaged and acted out. It is the engagement that moves this work from naming (nouning), to thinking about the possibility of ushering in much more (verbing).

Actors take on roles that are anterior to them. In taking on these roles they are supposed to enact the specific and particular requirements that are either documented by the playwright or commanded by the director. Actors perform the discourses of others as an other. Blackness as a discourse, when called up, uttered and performed, places the question of doing as central to what meanings might be derived from a set of actions. The temporality and spatiality of meaning as applied to blackness requires an acknowledgement of black cross-cultural resonances (creolization/hybridity). Thus place, space, and time are crucial to both black meanings and meanings of black. This migratory nature of "black meaning", of "black practices" that is, brings with it a specific historicity. Black positions which pay attention to gender and sexuality reveal that "no one is interested in telling the/truth" (26), as Brand puts it, and in the process articulate a new "truth" through a doubled gaze. That gaze is the cross-cultural resonance of Being.

What is at stake when black cultural studies addresses multiple singularities? What is at stake in coming to terms with what Mikhail Bakhtin calls "mutual liability to blame"? These questions remain unanswerable if we retain the idea of "unicultural" performance — identity as a tidy package of originary inheritances which reveal a specific core of familial bonds. Space and time, however, always reveal other traces. Edward Kamau Brathwaite's notion of the "tidal"[14] reveals that cultural practices, like waves, give, take and reshape, leaving new sediment behind in new forms. The arena of the political also suggests these complexities.

I insist upon working with questions of creolization and hybridity in order to try to understand what might be hopeful in a time when apocalyptic narratives are constantly being advocated. In this sense, my use of the postmodern does not signal a death of the author or subject but rather a proliferation of formerly discredited and subjugated knowledges and subjectivities.[15]

Sylvia Wynter, in "Beyond Miranda's Meanings: Un/silencing the 'Demonic Ground' of Caliban's 'Woman'"[16] suggests that we need to "point towards the epochal threshold of a new post-modern and post-Western mode of cognitive enquiry; one which goes beyond the limits of our present 'human sciences', to constitute itself as a new science of human 'forms of life'" (356). Wynter argues that Western and humanist notions impose the social categories of sex, gender, race, and sexuality as necessary for the present structures of power. Those structures, which prevent us from engaging with each other as human forms who cross-cut each other, are challenged in black feminist works, she argues. Wynter, in her readings of black women's texts, points us to the new possibilities: black feminist works occupy the in-between, they (re)theorize a universality that shifts us outside the discourse of ontology to dialogues concerning actions/practices and what those practices mean for the continuation of human life. It is no wonder that "mistaken identities"[17] can become "the laws" for reading black women's work. Their actions continually gesture to something more in their un/making of the "nounization" of the world.

Performing Language: The Performance of Language

Language can be said to structure one's relationship to the world.[18] It ordains the kinds of performances we are commanded to give in the context of our everyday lives. The use of language, therefore, is both a commonplace and a political act(ion). Words, Philip says, are not only actions; words act:

> the word
>   that claims
> and maims
>   and claims
> again
> (82).

While I am by no means suggesting that language is the only path to agency, it is almost inconceivable to think of agency outside of thinking about, and through, language. This is where language moves beyond mere words to sound off performative acts. In fact, language is a key to understanding black "conditions of servitude, oppression" and black responses and resistance to those conditions.[19] Language for diasporic black people is part and parcel of their resistance and reinvention of the self in the Americas, and this is especially true when the performative qualities of diasporic language become evident.

Resistance is clearly evident in the ways that black folks make language perform. Black language[20] not only works to convey and communicate ideas, it also works against the structures of domination by subverting overt meaning in performance. Black folks, then, do not only perform language, but their language is made to perform, to work in the service of revising and altering the wor(l)d.

How is it that various cultural resonances are both inflected and reflected in black language practices? Is language merely another invocation of black double consciousness and creolized cultural practices and forms? How is language tied to black identities as performative? I am not merely exploring the structures of language here; I am also suggesting that words constitute the performance of identities, communities and political acts. This is not only an exploration of the political act of black language, but also an exploration of how language impacts on politics and identity, as those elements are reflected in social and political culture. As Philip puts it in the introduction to *She Tries Her Tongue*, "language as we know it has to be dislocated and acted upon — even destroyed — so that it begins to serve our purposes" (19). She also argues that "[t]he havoc that the African wreaked upon English language is, in fact, the metaphorical equivalent of the havoc that coming to the New World represented for the African" (18). Clearly, it is at the interstices of dislocation, havoc and destruction that something new occurs.

Manthia Diawara has tried to make sense of this "something new" in the context of black cultural studies. In his "Black Studies, Cultural Studies: Performative Acts", he calls for a theory of black cultural studies which address the performative qualities of black expressive cultures. Diawara writes:

Black "performance studies" would mean study of the ways in which black people, through communicative action, created and continue to create themselves within the American experience. Such an approach would contain several interrelated notions, among them that "performance" involves an individual or group of people interpreting an existing tradition — reinventing themselves — in front of an audience, or public: and that black agency in the U.S. involves the redefinition of the tools of Americanness. Thus, the notion of "study" expands not only to include an appreciation of the importance of performative action historically, but also to include a performative aspect itself, a reenactment of a text or a style or a culturally specific response in a different medium (25).

Black language is particularly characteristic of the performative. It moves us far beyond notions of original, copy, and imitation to recognize black realities and "new origins". Black English speakers/users rewrite language and perform its deformation through an engagement with the practices of parody, deferral, bricolage, pastiche, collage, indirection, reversal and numerous other "postmodern practices"[21] to articulate and (re)invent representations and "I-mages" that push the limits of meaning(s). Philip borrows and shares i-mages as a word/sound with Rastafari, who in the Caribbean have waged a war on English, rewriting and subverting it so that the language can speak, write and (re)present their realities. Therefore Philip's argument that subversion has already happened to the language (19) is grounded in the practices of Caribbean realities. Possibilities, as well, lie in what the writer can do to, and with, the language in the name of creating new and just representations or "i-mages".

Parody is often one of the ways in which the creation of new representations is incubated. Judith Butler writes that parody can often call into question the very notion of the original (138). Black postmodern speech acts and language performance play with the notion of the original (if there is an original English at all), questioning origins while revealing the traces of residue from the "original" as important for the new invention. Butler further states that parody is not necessarily always subversive, but "what makes certain kinds of parodic repetitions effectively disruptive, truly troubling, [is that] repetitions become domesticated and rearticulated as instruments of cultural hegemony" (139); and these are important considerations for the politics of parodic black language play.

Repetition and parody are key to understanding black (re)writing of original signs and artifacts of the "master's" language and the laws of that language. Thus the performative acts of black language are a "dramatic and contingent construction of meaning" (Butler 139) that refuse to be pinned down for long periods of time. As Geneva Smitherman has pointed out, when the dominant culture takes up the use of black word meanings, black folk quickly change them (70). These practices signal the importance of fluidity to diasporic cultural practices.

Thus it is my contention that black word play is both reflective of black cultural politics and simultaneously an example of black cultural politics. The idea of the performative is a key to understanding both the limits and the excesses of black language performance and therefore its practices of resistance. Its continual (re)invention and (re)writing of a black self is performative in the senses that I am outlining here. The continued revision of words is one element of the performative in black language use. Philip's "Meditations on the Declension of Beauty by the Girl with Flying Cheekbones", for example, uses questioning to articulate black beauty:

> If not in yours
> In whose
> In whose language
> Am I
> If not in yours
> Beautiful
> (53).

Philip does not redefine words by inverting them (bad meaning good) in the usual diasporic manner. Instead, the "theory" and practice of inversion is embedded in her "rhetorical" questions concerning black beauty. The performance of her lyricism produces and/or uncovers black beauty. She turns the language on itself, calibanizing[22] it. Lines like "[w]oman with the behind that drives men mad"... and "[i]s the man with the full-moon lips/carrying the midnight of colour" (53) are political acts that recast racist tropes of black bodies. Put another way, Philip uses the language that makes black ugly not only to rescue black bodies, but also to re/make the black woman's and man's i-mage. Her crucial statement on i-mage is thus:

> history-
> the confusion of centuries that passes
> as the word
>   kinks hair
>   flattens noses
>   thickens lips
>   designs prognathous jaws
>   shrinks the brain
> to unleash the promise
>   in ugly
> the absent in image
> (78).

Culture, as Diawara suggests in his formulation of performative studies, is a citational, referential and resignificatory act. The same can obviously be said about language as a key component of culture. Conversely, black language takes its performative power from being able to reference and cite, in its reversal and subversions, the historical position of black diasporic peoples through allusions to the dominant meanings embedded in other uses of the words.

Philip's language draws on a historicity of black experiences and practices, but as Butler suggests, that historicity can never be fully disclosed. Thus Nourbese Philip makes language perform black historicity when she writes:

> insist upon it
> the evidence of newness
>   is
>   upon us
> without nigger slave coolie
> the wog of taint
> the word
> that in the beginning was
>   -not his
> I decree is mine
> (71).

Philip claims the word, that is English, as hers; fully gesturing to the context of black enslavement and Indian indentureship. This is a political act, for by claiming the word, Philip occupies an in-between space where her claims lead to something new.

The Repetitions of Language Practice

Dionne Brand uses repetition to rewrite "hegemonic and ambiguously hegemonic discourse". Her articulations of sexuality, of women loving women, are voiced in the repetitions of "this is your first lover, you/will never want to leave her" (46, 48, 51) a series of words which reveal the cartography of a new sexual practice for the narrator. Butler alerts us to the fact that performativity is primarily a discourse that only becomes actual when put into practice. "Performativity is not a singular 'act', for it is always a reiteration of the norm or set of norms, and to the extent that it requires an act-like status in the present, it conceals or dissimulates the conventions of which it is a repetition" (12). Brand's repetitions "normalize" lesbian sexuality in the context of a post-black nationalist feminist discourse. The citations and references that are the foundations of repetitions are what James Snead in "Repetition as a Figure of Black Culture" identifies as the sites that continually reproduce the circularity of black cultural expressions. Brand's use of repetition places her within the context of black cultural practices: she's drawing on aesthetic codes of presentation that signal an uneasy belonging. Her repetitions challenge any easy attempt to exclude black lesbians from postmodern blackness.

Consequently, black language as a method or way of knowing sets up the possibility for black people to engage cultural politics from the position that Cornel West calls a "critical organic catalyst" (33), while simultaneously resisting any form of what Frantz Fanon calls amputation (140). Black language works as both a method of renewal and as a link to a historical past that binds diasporic people within fluid communities. By this I mean to suggest that both Fanon's and West's interventions allow us to acknowledge sameness and to simultaneously acknowledge difference within. Brand brings a lesbian sexuality and desire to the question of identity as a critical organic catalyst and as a resistance to amputation. Thus thinking through the politics of black language can move us beyond what Diawara calls "oppression studies" (the study of racism and exclusion) to performative studies (the study of how black folk remake themselves and in the process remake entire societies). Clearly, one of the primary elements of performance studies is its polyphonic quality and black language is necessarily constituted as a polyphonic sounding.

Languishing Anguish: Living In-between

The "languishing" of both Philip and Brand is populated with irony. In "No Language is Neutral" Brand writes:

> Dumbfounded I walk as if these sidewalks are a
> place I'm visiting. Like a holy ghost I package the
> smell of zinnias and lady of the night, I horde the taste
> of star apples and granadilla...
> Ignoring
> my own money thrown on the counter, the race
> conscious landlords and their jim crow flats, oh yes!
> here! the work nobody wants to do...it's good
> work I'm not complaining! but they make it taste bad,
> bitter like peas...
> Our
> nostalgia was a lie and the passage on the six hour
> flight to ourselves is wide and like another world...
> (31-33).

Here she is performing the displacement of immigrantness and simultaneously addressing the complex issues of the in-between space alongside her own location in the national imagination. The narrator's memory makes her lie about her origins ("nostalgia was a lie"). At the same time, she's being told she doesn't 'belong' by landlords who position her outside the nation, and forced to accept employment no one else will take. These types of incidents compound, and represent the institutional practices of making blackness an absented presence;[23] or, as Brand puts it, "You the thin/mixture of just come don't exist" (29). Yet the narrator will "walk Bathurst Street until it come like home" (30) because she insists on her presence.

Thus, crucial to reading Philip's and Brand's poetry is the ironic, or what Linda Hutcheon calls the "splitting image"[24] of contemporary Canadian works. In black language use, English, the language of the dominator, is turned back on the master in recognition of anguish and then recouped, deformed and recast as resistance and renewal. In essence the laws are remade and the master disappears or is at least repositioned. Theirs is not a poetics of victimhood. Instead, Philip and Brand deform and (re)write the laws of the master; and in the process render law-making futile — because of the expressivity and performativity of blackness. In their words/language, blackness is construed as a fluid and tireless performance.

Where Brand's and Philip's work, and my analysis, departs from Hutcheon's (30), is in her tendency to define all immigrants vis-à-vis anglophone and francophone Canada. Hutcheon does not question the ways in which national narratives locate and position different immigrants into the imagined community of Canada. Brand's poetry, for example, performs the histories of diasporic black peoples and their cross-border journeys to North America:

> saying i
> coming just for holiday to the immigration officer when
> me and the son-of-a-bitch know I have labourer mark
> all over my face (29).

Language here charts black community through the experience of colonialism, imperialism and migration. The words do not and can not reveal the entire historicity of black exploitation in Canada, yet they reveal the traces, the contaminants, of black slave labour and black migrant labour histories. Thus when Hutcheon reads Dionne Brand alongside European migrants, she produces an ahistorical interpretation of Brand's performative use of English to convey the complex and contradictory relations of black migrancy.[25] Brand's words, indeed, call our attention to the question of the national imaginary. Both Brand and Philip make us perform, and in our performance acknowledge, that blackness cannot constitute Canadian-ness in contemporary nation-state narratives. What Brand's and Philip's poetry suggests to me is how the language used by diasporic black people references both their doubled existences, and also existences that refuse foundations. Or, as Edward Brathwaite has put it in another context, the language remains "fluid/tidal"[26] (Brathwaite develops a notion of tidalectics as opposed to dialectics, with the intent of finding metaphors from the Caribbean environment, and empowering those metaphors with meanings for articulating Caribbean realities) as it utters self and community.[27] The language performs its momentary specific historical context. Or as de Certeau puts it in regard to writing history: "[i]n organizing textual space, the structure establishes a contract and also orders social space. In this respect, the discourse does what it says. It is performative"(96).[28]

As a people in diaspora, migration/travel/exile is not an uncommon act or practice. It is, rather, the very way in which people live their lives and make their histories, everydays, futures and languages. Language can allow for a kind of reconnective remembering[29] of common experiences (i.e., resistance, pain) that conditions multiple forms of identification concerning the practices of domination and subordination for black people.

Language practices are often the spoken identificatory relations of community produced in the form of repetition. James Snead writes that: "black culture highlights the observance of such repetition, often in homage to an original generative instance or act" (218). Snead is specifically writing about cultural practices that, through their repetition by black diasporic people, demonstrate a relatedness and connectedness across boundaries. Brand, in the opening poem "Hard Against the Soul", uses repetition both to signal the beginning of each stanza and to make the reader (specifically female readers) understand that the poem is both for and about them. In repetition as well, she gestures to how racism, sexism and heterosexism as cultural practices render black women's experiences, and thus the naming of self, a difficult task:

> this is you girl, something never waning or forgetting
> something hard against the soul
> this is where you make sense, that the sight becomes
> tender, the night air human, the dull silence full
> chattering, volcanoes cease, and to be awake is
> more lovely than dreams (7).

For as Sylvia Wynter points out, black women's writing has moved us beyond "all our present theoretical models in their 'pure' forms, based on their isolated 'isms', has enabled the move, however preliminary, on to the 'demonic' and now unsilencing trans-'isms' ground of Caliban's woman" (366). Brand's simultaneous grappling with racism, sexism and heteronormativity constitutes the preliminary unsilencing of "trans-isms".

The performative qualities of language and, in this case, resisting subjects, are crucial to the political acts of Brand and Philip. They remake, or rather *alter*, language to make it perform the acts of their politics. Philip alters the notion of "bloodcloth" to reclaim it as a sign for mature womanhood and to articulate a black female self. Brand, on the other hand, reworks words like "guerillas" to make them perform the experience and interior life of the poem's narrator. She writes, "I saw your back arched against this city we inhabit like guerillas." In this context, her riffing evokes the idea of guerillas as warriors for justice as well as racist notions of black people being genealogically linked to the ape family. As Michael Taussig would say, Philip and Brand occupy "a space permeated by the colonial tension of mimesis and alterity, in which it is far from easy to say who is the imitator and who is imitated, which is copy and which is original" (78). Their language performances are clearly an engagement with the historicity of black diasporic memory, remembering, and experience of colonialism and imperialism, and what it means to alter those incursions.

Altered Identities

Black language usage might constitute what Sigmund Freud called "common feeling" — common feeling because the language is not a glue but rather much more like a lubricant: the language practice insists on moving outside of stasis and in the direction of verbing. Common feeling signals the slip of mimesis that can lead to the alterability of post-colonial and postmodern blackness in intrablack and extrablack dialogues. Common feeling is part of the dispersed re-connection with the self, and black language brings into being the politics for reinventing the self and resisting domination simultaneously.

Both Philip and Brand chart a racialized, gendered, sexualized history of the black diaspora that moves between the cartographies of "race", "gender", "sex" and "space" to reconfigure and (re)chart black diasporic political identifications at the dawn of the twenty-first century. The dialogue and conversation concerning post-colonial and postmodern blackness is one of fluidity, which does not negate the continuing practices of nation-state oppression, but instead riffs off of that oppression. These poetic works, however, move beyond the discourses of victimhood to resist amputations and to plot and chart the coordinates for a new exodus, one that's embedded with the possibilities of freedom.

Black Subjectivities
Ethnicity, Race and the Politics of Film in Canada

So that my own aesthetic formulation for ourselves begins with rhythm: survival rhythm, emancipation rhythm, transfiguration rhythm; and how the one, the ego, comes to this, comes out of this, relates to this and us and others (Edward Kamau Brathwaite 65).

The goal is not to replace bad old negative images with new good positive images. Work on stereotyping has outlined the danger in bringing evaluative criteria such as comparing characters in "real life" to discern the presence of stereotyping. The relation to "the real" or an "ideal" does not designate whether stereotyping is manifest. It is, however, as Steve Neale argues, repetition, *repetition without difference, which underwrites the process.* Racism is not located within the text, it is determined by the discourses which surround it, its context. *Overly formulaic scripts, coupled with familiar clichés, effect determinist narratives* (Kass Banning 19).

In 1996, Canada, or more specifically Toronto, was treated to five days of relentless media coverage concerning a young black man. It was not because of a sporting event: no, Donovan Bailey had not broken yet another world sprint record. Instead, it was that other "racial stew" that the North American media loves so much — black and criminal. Adrian Mathias Kinkead's face graced every newspaper and television news program in the country. A black "serial killer" on the loose screamed some of the headlines. Stretching the definition of serial killer to fit Kinkead, accused of killing three people, had to be done in light of the boy-next-door atrocities of Paul Bernardo, a white "native son".[1] But had that been the only reason that Kinkead made the news, my retelling of this narrative would be useless. Kinkead was not only named as black and criminal but as black, *Jamaican* and criminal. This designation holds important consequences in the public discourses of law and order and its Canadian twin, immigrantness. Jamaicans have been "marked" as the most violent and criminal among black immigrants in Canada, and a reverse migration (deportation) back "home", after doing time for their crimes, has been inaugurated.

Just as disturbing was another report in Canada's and Toronto's most notoriously racist tabloid which announced in a front page headline: "Jamaicans jeer Ranger out". Rohan Ranger, the cousin of Adrian Kinkead, was linked to two of the murders; he took refuge in Jamaica either because of his guilt or to hide from the trigger-happy Toronto police. The fear of being shot is real. Over the last decade the police in Toronto have killed no fewer than nine black men and severely wounded one black woman, paralyzing her — and no one has been disciplined for these acts.[2] All of the shootings took place within the context of highly suspect practices on the part of the police — both before and after the incidents.

The tensions surrounding police violence have found their way into black Canadian artistic expression — film, theatre, literature, poetry and music in particular.

Recent forays into feature film by two black filmmakers use the existing tensions of criminal activity in black communities and police harassment to chart a cinematic language of blackness in Canada. I would suggest that this is a rather easy and slightly unimaginative place to begin to map blackness in the country and one that can only lead to a morass of realist cinema[3] that elides the complexities of black communities. Using a formula that borrows heavily from African-American hood films, the narratives attempt to reproduce "the real" and posit a limited, masculinized, heterosexist narrative of blackness in Canada.[4] The first two black Canadian feature films — Stephen Williams' *Soul Survivor* and Clement Virgo's *Rude*[5] — are concerned primarily with the "emasculating" forces in black men's lives at the expense of the ways in which black people fashion individual and collective selves and communities in the context of various forms of domination within and against the nation-state of Canada.

Theorizing Black Canadian

The complex realities of black community in Canada have not yet been mapped in any critical cinematic way. Selina Williams' *Saar* merely hinted at the complexity by gathering a diasporic black female community. Colina Philips' *Making Change* is another important film which takes an entirely different direction (see the discussion of this film in chapter 7). My desire for complexity, however, makes me return to the Dream Warriors' musical announcement about their planned "voyage through the multiverse". The Dream Warriors have acknowledged the multiple positionalities of black diasporic peoples in their lyrics. And ultimately, I think that the metaphoric and symbolic moment of a multiverse is particularly significant not only for music, but also for the development of a black Canadian cinema.

Such an argument calls for a contextualization of who the black Canadian might be. How do we understand who the black Canadian is? What is black Canadian community(ies) and what constitutes black Canadian expressive cultures? Addressing these questions goes a long way in helping us make sense of what is required of a cinema that speaks the past, present and future of black Canadian identities and identifications.

If definitions of black Canadian are centred around political practices/act(ion)s that signal a transgression of instituted forms and practices of domination, then black Canadian might be anyone who resists in concerted ways, with a vision of emancipation, all forms of domination. Black Canadian is a counter-narrative or utterance that calls into question the very conditions of nation-bound identity at the same time as national discourses attempt to render blackness outside the nation.[6] My articulation of black Canadian will undoubtedly leave some feeling that the borders are open, an invitation to all. In many ways they are. What I am after is the attempt to articulate, and struggle to create, a space that acknowledges transgressing the "usual and assumed" as an important practice of the political. My questions are not meant to stifle creative and imaginative works of art. So to get at some sense of what those questions suggest, and require of us, I will look at Stephen Williams's *Soul Survivor*.

To be clear I want to theorize black Canadian as wholly outside the biological and the national. Black Canadian is for me syncretic, always in revision and in a process of becoming. It is constituted from multiple histories of uprootedness, migration, exchanges and political acts of defiance and self-

(re)definition. I use the "archaic" and "ancient" term "black" as a way of framing the political discourse that I am constructing here. I am attempting to formulate an understanding of political acts that go beyond linear, narrow and rigid narratives of identity that are organized around origin as founded in Africa and thus constituting the cultural identity of black-skinned peoples. Such positions still carry great sway in contemporary discourse, but as Stuart Hall notes: "Cultural identities are the points of identification, the unstable points of identification or suture, which are made within the discourse of history and culture" (224). The discourse of blackness allows for understanding identity as practices of identification used to revise and creolize who we are. *Soul Survivor* lacks an historical, or rather, a temporal context for its narrative.

Listening To Film

Williams's use of reggae in his soundtrack and narrative could be seen as a signal of black diasporic cultural identities if it was used as a locus for diasporic identification. A DJ opens *Soul Survivor* announcing the next tune/song to be played and this cinematic riff returns me to Paul Gilroy's (1993) injunction that music characterizes almost everything cultural about black life. Because music is immediately central to the film, Williams signals spaces for the introduction of specific identities and sites for multiple identifications. The fact that rooted identity quickly becomes the focal point of *Soul Survivor* is one of its weaknesses.

Williams's use of reggae as a structuring device is important because he does not use music to open diasporic dialogue but rather as a marker for heritage. The only migration that reggae makes for Williams's narrative is to announce a black Jamaican difference in a hellish Canada. Reggae works as a fetishized object and foundation for marking, maintaining and securing the protagonist's Canadian identity. It is the signal that names him Jamaican, but never, in this film, does it reference a sonic diaspora.

The Politics of Naming

Two black men (Stephen Williams and Clement Virgo) make feature films, and the discourse of black Canadian as identity marker — and more importantly as mapping the complex processes of blackness in Canada — disappears from discussion of the films. In the "Festival" issue of *Take One* both *Soul Survivor* and *Rude* are discussed and named simultaneously as "Jamaican-Canadian" movies.[7] I find this curious. What does this return to ethnic particularity suggest about blackness and its semiotic chain of meanings here? What are we to understand by the term "black Canadian" and for whom is it reserved? As is often the case with films that seek to explore the complex politics of identity, *Soul Survivor* finds itself being more concerned with root and origin, rather than with "seeing identity as a process of movement and meditation that is more appropriately approached via the homonym routes" (Gilroy 19). The assertion by film critics that we now have a "Jamaican-Canadian", as opposed to a black Canadian filmic identity, renders invisible the complex processes of how various moments and forms of blackness become and are becoming in Canada.

To label these films as "Jamaican-Canadian" draws on multicultural narratives of heritage which are concerned with origin and tend to occlude the complex creolized multicultural constitution of black Canadians. Yet a Canadian multicultural desire for simplicity and knowability is revealed in the naming. In Canada, black identities must be rooted elsewhere and that elsewhere is always outside Canada. Black subjects become knowable objects through a simple, uncomplicated story of origins.[8]

But the naming spells more than that, because it puts into place a semiotics of meanings. The naming triggers a chain of meanings that are associated with assumed actions and specific identities in Canada. It is the desire to pin down identity as knowable and explainable that makes the compound "Jamaican-Canadian" meaningful and common-sensical to critics. In recent interviews with both Williams and Virgo, therefore, biography has been of central importance.

The prevalence of this information is important because their narratives' realism is supposed to offer an authentic peep into the world that might help us to understand, or at least get a handle on, the Kinkeads and Rangers who roam Canada's housing projects. Biographical curiosity points to how film critics and others use these films to pathologize immigrant Jamaicans and render them knowable and explainable. To an assumed white "mainstream" audience they are representative of the Canadian exotic, victim, "underclass" thing. If such a reading seems harsh, I only need to remind you that the Toronto Police Services Board intended in 1991 to use African-American John Singleton's *Boyz 'N' the Hood* as a training video for its officers.[9] Canada's racialized immigrant mythology is dependent upon narratives that riff off of the nation's discourse of benevolence and goodness towards immigrants, but simultaneously places those immigrants within a crippling discourse of heritage that locates non-white others outside of the nation. *Soul Survivor* does not question the discourse of heritage; in fact Williams's earlier film, *Variation On A Key 2 Life*, is even more steeped in this discourse: the male protagonist is caught up in the claws of "anxiety and alienation" in Canada and can only escape with music (he is a saxophone player) and women.

Mapping the Identity of a *Soul Survivor*

Jerry Gafio Watts writes of the "victim status syndrome", which he believes can be "a useful mechanism for inducing white guilt" (19). Victim status syndrome tends to dominate the narratives of "hood" films. In *New Jack City*, *Juice*, *Straight Out of Brooklyn*, *Boyz 'N' the Hood*, *Menace II Society* and so on, renderings of blackness as victim, criminal and masculinized have been privileged by both the white and black middle class as representative of the totality of blackness. The filmmakers all construct black patriarchal "heroic transcendence"[10] as the site or avenue to emancipation and/or survival for black people. That is, by the end of these films, the narratives suggest men are solely responsible for black community. In these narratives of blackness, black women, gays, lesbians and anyone who does not toe the line of narrowly defined blackness are considered unimportant. A counter to these films' narratives would be the black Canadian "soul survivors" who revise and creolize identity and identifications for continued survival as acts to emancipate the self.

Soul Survivor does not engage the diasporic connectedness and rhizomatic character of blackness in the Canadian context (there are a few hints — an African immigrant family is one of the indebted families), but instead insists on an immigrant "underclass" representation which clouds Canadian complexities of blackness. The underclass representation points to the limits of the film's narrative for expressions of blackness in Canada. I would suggest that this representation fits into a transglobal semiotics of blackness as a sign of victimization, where blacks are victims of white racism, struggling to be free in the centre of a white hell. Of course, such renditions of blackness might signal a "truth" for some, but in the realm of cinematic representations this kind of narrative fits neatly within a paradigm of recent and current "hood" films that render blackness one-dimensionally as being involved in what C.L.R. James refers to as "the struggle for happiness".

The struggle for happiness presented in these "hood" films constantly depicts blackness in relation to a dominating and controlling whiteness; and even though these films carry a strong sense of a black aesthetic, and aural practices that massage the senses, they do not construct black selves in the ways that jazz, blues, reggae and calypso historically have. That is, these films, despite overtures that suggest self-definition, do not render complex discussions of black life.

So this is where I differ with Toronto film critics who have read these films, and in particular *Soul Survivor*, as significantly different from African-American "hood" films. *Soul Survivor* is the Canadian realist version of the currently commodified transglobal renderings of blackness as violent, criminal and "underclass". While it is always possible to read these films as demonstrating the processes of racism in North American urban centres, and I believe that such readings are a crucial element of both the intent and narratives of the films, nonetheless the films also posit an "economy of race" that does not challenge current dominant symbolic orders of what sells as blackness cinematically.

Soul Survivor's Plot

In Williams's *Soul Survivor* the main character Tyrone (Peter Williams), is tormented by his "struggle for happiness". Tyrone's struggle resides in his desire to own and operate a small restaurant that plays the latest reggae tunes. Music continually marks a nostalgia for a mythic home, but again, as Dionne Brand puts it in *No Language is Neutral*, "nostalgia was a lie" (33). Williams continually links music to his cinematic narrative of identity and displacement. Racism is the obstacle that prevents Tyrone from achieving his desires. It seems that the only possible way out is to become employed by Winston (George Marks), who runs a menacing semi-legal business, but even more importantly, represents the patriarchal black father figure. Looking up to Winston raises important ethical issues for Tyrone, since Winston represents both what Tyrone would like to be (wealthy) and what Tyrone does not want to be (criminal). Tyrone is caught at a dangerous crossroad. One foot rests on the dark doorstep of the criminal underworld, while his other foot guides him to the torturous avenue of Canadian racism which forced him into the situation with Winston in the first place. Tyrone is a victim: one we are supposed to both pity and identify with as a casualty of racism.

Tyrone becomes Winston's debt collector, and he does the job all too well. A generous reading of the film might argue that Tyrone represents the African god Esu[11] — with one foot in this world and one foot in the world of the gods. His miraculous escape from the white racist tenants whose money he takes for Winston, is a case in point. As well, the repeated shots of the small African mask hanging around his neck are an indication and invocation of the divine qualities that Tyrone possesses. He is a walking, talking version of Du Boisian doubleness. It is the limitations of that doubleness that I question.

A black Canadian process of identification would instead centre black people in a temporal and spacial narrative that highlights both struggle and resistance, and demonstrates that shaping and (re)shaping both identity and Canada must be achieved through political actions and doings. Black Canadian, as name/metaphor for the rhythms of black migration, would disrupt the ethnic absolutist claim to blackness as sign of oppression, and recast blackness as performative.[12]

One of the important roles for Tyrone is to protect and shadow his cousin and friend, Rueben (David Smith) — and this is another example of his divine qualities. Rueben is portrayed as an "irresponsible" Rastafarian musician who owes Winston five thousand dollars and is reckless about repayment. Rueben often acts on impulse rather than reason, and is continually referred to as childish, crazy or mad. Only the impotent Papa (Ardon Bess) thinks he is smart. Rueben eventually organizes a retaliatory strike which is meant to bring Winston, the "Babylon Vampire", down. The strike leads to Rueben's murder and Tyrone's only lapse into impotency.

Beyond the Soft Dick Syndrome

It is my contention that "hood" films are premised on the idea that representations of blackness make sense in an economy of "underclass", black (immigrant) male impotency. Hood films riff off of the old paradigms of the Black Arts Movement. Their narratives are preoccupied with (re)gaining manhood for black men. Consequently, it is the regaining of black male potency that all these "hood" films explore and seek to (re)place and (re)settle as fundamental to the survival of both the self and black communities. The impotent black man in *Soul Survivor* is best represented by Papa. In every frame but one Papa is shown prone, dependent on Grandma (Leonie Frobes) for assistance of some kind. He is rendered impotent by the racism of Canadian labour practices. After having worked long hours at "shit jobs", he is of no use to himself and his family, for as Winston says, "a man has to look after his family". In fact, Grandma now has the upper hand. This once strong man must now "lovingly" pay her for his rum, and matches to light his cigarettes.

Tyrone must define himself vis-à-vis this impotent father figure who was once a trade unionist, a socialist in Jamaica, and "defender of the small man". Winston, who tells us that money is everything, becomes the more appropriate stand-in, the father figure Tyrone must emulate and take advice from. Winston's role represents all that is bourgeois Canada, warning that you can only be on the inside when you have money: "You're nothing without money, you're not inside you're outside". This epitomizes the struggle for happiness.

Williams's narrative partially represents a liberatory project for blackness. *Soul Survivor* renders black women mute, because they represent the lack against which black men must continually regain their potency in the midst of racism and exclusion from capitalist patriarchy. In particular, Tyrone's relationship with Annie (Judith Scott) maps the disenfranchisement of black women from liberatory narratives of blackness. The film hints that Tyrone's relationship with Annie went sour because he abused her. In one important scene following an example of police brutality, Annie asserts herself as Rueben's caseworker, and Tyrone says to her "You been away too long, forgot what it like". Tyrone does this in the midst of the two most debilitating threats to his manhood — the police, and dominating, educated black women with jobs, like Annie.[13] She is implicitly accused of forgetting family connections (and indeed, in the film she has none) when Tyrone asserts that he has to look after Rueben. This is the recurring contemporary (urban) tale of black women's desertion of black men. The narrative of the film offers no information on Annie and how she became a caseworker, with all the trappings of middle-class success, but we get the indication that she might be "a ball-breaker" when she says to Tyrone, "You think you fly". Black women constitute a part of the emasculating apparatus of black men. Annie, however, must eventually come around, or, like the love interest in *Variation*, she will be replaced with another woman.

After The Seduction of Some Black Aesthetic Practices

What makes many of these "hood" films appear to be "authentic" representations of blackness are the ways in which black cultural practices are imported into them as occasions for evoking identification. From confrontations with police, to hairstyles, to proverbs, these films are packed with numerous elements of "black" everyday living. *Soul Survivor* makes use of language, vibrant colours, the playing of dominoes, styles of dress, posture and jewellery to etch a black aesthetic. Winston's hangout, "The Black Star Line", references Marcus Garvey and raises numerous issues too voluminous to discuss here. But one question remains: Are they hanging out in a sinking black ship? Foundational identity claims are usually linked to death. The film's aesthetic practices are not a signal of diasporic connectedness, but rather they become a part of the continuing catalogue of rootedness that makes this film fit into the discourse of heritage and origin.

Again, one of the challenging aesthetic features of *Soul Survivor* is how intrinsic music is to the narrative. Rastas and music, in particular reggae, are indelibly inscribed and linked. Not merely because Rueben is a musician, but also in the ways Williams uses music as voice-over to bring rhythm to the film and chart the theme of survival. Williams's rhythm, however, is not an emancipation rhythm or a transfiguration rhythm as Brathwaite would have it. Yes, Rueben's death announces what happens to one's culture in "a land of strangers", as Papa says. And ideas of immigrant culture dying and withering away in the midst of victimization are standard and easy narratives to tap into and use to define and name. But to acknowledge revisions and changes, to incorporate the dynamism of cultural practices, is much more difficult and challenging.

Soul Survivor ends with Annie coming to Tyrone's side to sit with him on the step. Grandma continues to play the lottery despite Rueben's death and Papa remains impotent and prone in bed. A haunting and loud rendition of Bob Marley's "Redemption Song" plays. The filmic image is one of Annie's subjugation to both Tyrone's desire and his need to assert and fashion a manhood that looks after his family. For the first time Tyrone is not standing above everyone, but significantly too, his manhood is affirmed when Annie symbolically and literally comes down to his level. As a victim of racism and "brothers jacking other brothers", Tyrone's only response in this film is to survive. Marley's "Redemption Song" becomes a wail for the continued impotence and death of the black man. "How long shall they kill our prophets while we stand aside and look" makes history and identity an issue of life and death.

Rueben's death signals the toll of victimhood in the film. Rueben, as artist/musician and Rastafari, potentially represents one of the most complex characters in the film. Yet the narrative fails him. Williams is unable to deliver on this potential because he does not make use of reggae and Rastafari culture as diasporic sites for identification, sharing, and dialogue, but rather as markers of a Jamaican-ness that Canadian national discourses of multiculturalism insist specific groups claim. Rastas and reggae become the crown jewels of the heritage discourse. And thus the film's narrative leaves Rueben locked in displacement: he exists between ethnicity and nation, and this can only be crippling and eventually lead to his death.

Rueben's character is antithetical to what occurs when Rastafari ideology migrates. Rastas everywhere, while paying homage to Jamaican Rastafarians, revise and rewrite Rastafari culture to make it applicable to their localities. Ras Rueben, cinematically, is locked in an archaicizing discourse, and this leaves his character little room to manoeuvre.

When I return to the Dream Warriors and the fluidity that they and their music represent and present, I find there is an un/conscious play with, and of, identity. Using naming and the types of music they sample (reggae, calypso, jazz, game show theme songs), the Dream Warriors create multiple sites for identification for their audiences. Black Canadian cinema might need to turn to music(ians) as a site for the exploration of a dialogue that might enhance the measure of the discourse concerning ethnicity, race and belonging in Canada.

Sylvia Wynter, in arguing for new ways of thinking through the politics and practice of aesthetics in literary and film criticism, states: "The proposal here is that these processes of positive/negative marking which enact/inscribe the code of 'life' and 'death' are always initiated by the *narratives of origin* from which all such codes and, therefore, their 'paradigms of value and authority' are brought to 'birth' (251; emphasis in the original). Marley's "Redemption Song" works to make the narrative of black/immigrant victimization in *Soul Survivor* complete. By doing so, film critics can assert a naming of the film as Jamaican-Canadian because the "paradigms of value and authority", which give "birth" to narratives of immigrants and blacks as victims, fits within a paradigmatic transglobal frame for reading blackness. Marley, Rastas, Black Star Line, in this film do not reference the diasporic sharing that these symbols have come to represent. Instead, they are markers for origins: roots that eventually wither and die in a "stranger land".[14]

Black Canadian, as a name, would complicate the neat packaging of blackness that film critics need. Because when diasporic sharing, dialogue, exchange, connectedness and syncretism are not subsumed in a film's narrative, critics will be required to move beyond the too easy linear structures for locating rooted aesthetic practices as signposts for identity.

The pedagogy of *Soul Survivor*, however, leaves us with a narrative that suggests all black men want to do is to look after their families. This might be read in the context of the opening voice-over where Tyrone asserts that, "In this life it's not about collecting other people's debts, it's about paying for your own". Rueben dies because he cannot pay Winston and Tyrone survives as the embodiment of a "heroic transcendent" black man continually suffering and surviving "against all odds". Tyrone's conservative voice-over, however, has other implications in the context of Canada's discourse of heritage. "Paying for your own" is echoed in nation-state policies concerning roots and origins so that the Kinkeads and Rangers of the north will signify, when they are deported to Jamaica, Canada's return of the repressed.

Scattered Speculations on Canadian Blackness; Or, Grammar for Black

I

The dearth of debate concerning "ways of thinking" blackness in Canada should not be surprising. To continually return to music as a major feature of black diasporic cultural expression and identity and as one of its fundamental structuring devices might be clichéd, yet music remains one of the most complex and significant expressive cultural forms of the black diaspora. Other imaginative works like literature and film have played an important and ground-breaking role in providing other avenues for representing the complexities of black life in the Americas. I return to music because it signals an important, shared, and continually reinvented black diasporic expression. I believe that music in Canada provides an outlet that allows us to chart the various ways in which black Canadian cultures can be understood and engaged.

The Dream Warriors and Maestro Fresh-Wes might best support my claims. These Canadian musicians have taken different diasporic paths and created different identifications as their careers have taken off, ebbed and flowed. The Dream Warriors have returned in their music to a much closer identification with the Caribbean, particularly Jamaica. Fresh-

Wes, on the other hand, has clearly identified with America; he has even moved to New York. The migratory practices suggest that avenues for thinking about blackness by black Canadians do not follow a single path. While I have paid attention to how the films of Stephen Williams and Clement Virgo draw on the African-American hood film genre, it is equally important, especially in the case of Virgo, to recognize and account for black British cinematic influences and references. These cross-border or outer-national identifications are what constitute the complex nature of black identifications in Canada. The debate has, however, failed to acknowledge this.

It seems imperative, then, that when we theorize black Canadas, that diasporic exchanges, dialogues and renewals become a fundamental part of thinking what the politics of blackness might be. Once the processes of invention and reinvention are highlighted and dealt with, much more complex analyses can come into play. These analyses allow for, and result in, the pluralizing of blackness. Therefore, reading blackness both as a sign and as performative, through a method of nomadology, might be a useful way of thinking about black cultures in Canada. Nomadology (see chapter 4) is the attempt to think about movement and exile in a fashion which makes those conditions a part of the way in which cultural work is understood and valued.

II

Consequently, it would be silly to be offended by Andre Alexis suggesting, in *This Magazine*, that blackness in Canada is "borrowed". Blackness is always borrowed. What is really at stake is what is done with borrowed blackness. Alexis's claim, that not enough Canadian artists, choreographers, painters and thinkers writing from here write about "our" specificities, however, is suspect. He argues that black culture in Toronto is disproportionately influenced by African-American culture. But his logic would probably be unable to account for the Dream Warriors' "return" to the Caribbean or the influence of Black British film in Clement Virgo's work.

Instead, Alexis offers some cursory readings of African-American cultural criticism and theory: relying heavily on Cornel West, in particular, he suggests that black Canadian-ness is fashioned after African-American-ness. His reliance on West would suggest to those not conversant with the debates that there was no debate concerning West's ideas among African-Americans. This is far from the truth. But if black Canadian "loudness", concerning matters of "race" is bor-rowed from an African-American model it seems clear that black Canadians reinvent what they borrow for local purpos-es. For while it might be argued that in some limited sense Alexis has a point, his refusal to seriously engage the condi-tions of black diasporic identifications is puzzling.

African-American history and experience is surely not archetypal nor exceptional from where I stand. Yet, it can not be denied that the fate of the world's black peoples is some how linked to the ways in which Americans export and practice their ideas of racial supremacy. What is crucially important is that we recognize that discourses of race are not merely nation bound, but that they also cut across nations. Similarly, those who are oppressed understand their experi-ences both locally and extralocally. Black people in Canada can and do identify with black people in the Caribbean, Brazil, South Africa, America and the rest of the world; and such identifications are valid. These identifications are the stuff of which the conditions for a nomadology of blackness is constituted.

My insistence on border-crossing identifications is not just some postmodern collage, a construct that makes space and place loosely interchangeable; instead this is how black (post)modernity makes crucial links, across national space, to demonstrate some of the ways in which black people sometimes share pain, pleasure, disappointments and hope. Alexis's inability to access such understandings, to know why those identifications assert themselves as black commonalities, explains why he fails to acknowledge what it means to be "at home" in Canada.

To be black and "at home" in Canada is both to belong and not belong. The Dream Warriors celebrate black diasporic connectedness and passion in their song "Ludi" by calling out and naming black home spaces in Canada and the Caribbean. The practice is a practice of the in-between. It is from a life at, or on, the in-between space that Dionne Brand, M. Nourbese Philip, Austin Clarke, Cecil Foster, George Elliott Clarke, Claire Harris, Frederick Ward, and a host of other writers, thinkers, dramatists, choreographers, musicians, film-makers (and Alexis himself) articulate: a political and ethical stance which refuses the too-easy boundaries of national discourses. Calls for justice in their work are not ill-informed, naive rants, but rather they speak to "instilling pride in *this* place" (Alexis 18; emphasis in original). Nation-centred discourse can only be a trap that prohibits black folks from sharing "common feeling", especially when common actions and practices of domination seem to present themselves time and again in different spaces/places/nations.

Alexis hints at the complex manifestations of blackness in Canada, but undermines the very argument he intends to make when he does not discuss how black cultures, especially Caribbean cultures, are over-policed in this place. Yes, it is

true that calypso, cricket and reggae as well, have reshaped
Toronto and Canada. But these kinds of things do so at the
expense of rendering more invisible long-standing black communities in Ontario, Nova Scotia, Quebec, British Columbia
and the Western provinces. Watching cricket in King City or
at Ross Lord Park, black bodies and other bodies of colour
actually and symbolically refigure Canadian space and make
their presence felt beyond the confines and restrictions of
immigration legislation, multicultural discourse and policies,
and the local police. Resorting to what gets read as recent
immigrant contributions to the Canadian cultural landscape
in the popular imagination does not bring us any closer to
articulating an "indigenous black" discourse around race,
space, and nation — a discourse which will allow us to
understand the ways in which blackness remakes the
Canadian political, cultural and literary landscape.

On the one hand, black folks here are told that any political
and social identification with African-Americans is wrong-
headed and over-determined (Alexis); and on the other hand,
forms of criticism uniquely located in Canadian contexts are
undermined by dismissals of anger. Michael Coren's unwar-
ranted and misguided attack on M. Nourbese Philip is a case
in point. And yet, Alexis' fine collection of short stories,
Despair, is itself evidence of an attempt to invent a Canadian
blackness. His stories are representative of a black Canadian-
ness constituted from various fragments of the nation, usually
seen as outside blackness. The existence of Alexis's short sto
ries both support and simultaneously deny his argument
because they stand out as distinct from the usual fare, and
exist as a "voice" of black Canadian difference and plurality.
In the same way, George Elliott Clarke's poetic works should
be noted for their Nova Scotian cadences, histories, utter-

ances, and the ways in which the poems disturb a white Canadian normativity by placing blackness at the centre of their Canadian-ness.

Incidentally, when African-American as a symbolic category of authenticity works in favour of the dominant discourse it is called on to discredit local articulations and concerns. The hiring and invitation of Henry Louis Gates Jr. by Garth Drabinsky's Livent Corporation to act as both consultant and spokesman for quelling the black resistance to mounting *Showboat* at a publicly funded arts space in 1993 is just one example. Middle-class African-American comfort and nostalgia with the staging of *Showboat* in New York was used to make black Canadian concerns seem ridiculous. In this case, the dominant discourse believed it was valid to make sense of blackness in Canada through African-American response and experience.[1] Black Canadian assertions of commonality with African-Americans, however, were denied.

III

Significantly, Andrew Moodie's award-winning play *Riot* offers a complex range of black characters and black cultures. The play's insistence on clearly marking out black difference across history, gender, sex, class, sense of belonging, desire and ambition, though at times didactic, opens up a dialogue of the impossible: a singular blackness in Canada. Moodie's contribution to black Canadian theatre should usher in an era when uncritical black affirmative works (with few exceptions many short film and videos provide this kind of fare) are not the only ones which grace the stages.

Because black differences are accentuated in *Riot*, the audience views a complex dynamic of cultures and the consequences and dynamics of life which allow for thinking blackness as multiple. The drama of the play makes clear and evident the multi-accentuality of racism while simultaneously addressing the crossing of racism with other social and cultural forms of discrimination like homophobia. *Riot* then moves the expressive cultural production of black Canadas from works which desire a black sameness and singularity to a "new" and different place. In the aftermath of *Riot* we must ask: What conditions make a black community?

IV

The song "My Definition" by the Dream Warriors does not offer a lyrical definition of blackness. In fact, the definition is offered in the method of the song. Not unlike Alexis's *Despair*, the Dream Warriors draw from fragments of the nation to make and invent Canadian blackness. By that I mean that the Dream Warriors' reappropriation of the game show *Definition*'s theme song signals the way in which they understand themselves as embedded in the Canadian body politic, and what they can take from it. Their use of the song disrupts a white Canadian normativity and recasts it in its black history by effectively quoting its black composer, Quincy Jones.

We are therefore faced with the question: What grammars of black exist in Canada for locating black people as central to the nation? How can we articulate a recent migratory history alongside a much longer black presence? How do we articulate the continuous and continuing post-World War II migrations (a continuous history of migration) alongside the pre-war migrations and the migrations of the periods of settlement (a discontinuous history of migration)? Thinking carefully about a Canadian grammar for black might help us to avoid the painful and disappointing moments of an essentialized blackness.

A discourse and grammar for blackness in Canada can be

located at the interstices of various histories of migration. The history of ex-slaves in what is now called Canada — black loyalists both slave and free; fugitive slaves from the U.S.; pre and post-emancipation Caribbean migrants; late nineteenth century and early twentieth century migrants — constitutes a discontinuous history of black migration to Canada. The decendents of these early migrants are scattered across Canada but concentrations exist in Nova Scotia and Ontario. A continuous migration is characterized by post-World War II migration from the Caribbean, and more recent but dwindling migrations from the African continent and other black spaces. The most recent migrations have taken precedence in the popular imagination and therefore authorities tend to locate blackness as "new" to the nation. However, black people need to figure out how to produce the tensions and possibilities of these two migratory moments in a way which recognizes a long and enduring presence in Canada.

If black Canadians can learn anything from African-Americans it is how to "invent" and continually reference a "tradition". The process is important, not the content. George Elliott Clarke's *Fire on the Water (volume 1)* presents some of the figures whom might be used to invent and continually reference a malleable black Canadian "tradition". David George, Carrie M. Best, Pearleen Oliver, and those who are not in the anthology (Mary Anne Shadd, Mary Bibb, and a host of others), are important starting points in archiving black Canadian histories. The stories we tell, and the "myths" we create, produce an antidote to what Clarke terms "the struggle against erasure" in *Eyeing the North Star*.

Therefore, a grammar for black must ground itself in a long black history. The almost five-hundred-year presence of black people in Canada should not merely be an item in the catalogue of blackness: it should be actively used to inform the ways in which we analyze the nation and our citizenship.

V

In this regard, my thoughts on Colina Philips's *Making Change* might be seen as a reading of her film which both sets up the ground and inaugurates the possibility of thinking about the complexities of blackness in Canada. *Making Change* is an eighteen-minute cinematic "riffology" and "sound sculpture" (Troupe 87) which was released the same year as *Rude* and *Soul Survivor*. *Making Change* is a marked departure for black Canadian film that has been little discussed, even in the context of the minuscule attention that black film receives. Leslie Sanders's "Anti/Modern Spaces: African Canadians in Nova Scotia" is the only essay which discusses the film and places its theme within the framework for thinking about modern Canadian spaces and the discourses of blackness. The film's cinematic textuality and texture exist somewhere between the modern and the postmodern as the filmmaker works both sites/cites to narrate a tale of the black Canadian "distilled history of memory" (Troupe 90). *Making Change* is contradictorily a silent film, because an original jazz score accompanies it and works as the speaking voice of the actors.

The opening scene of the film features a black woman (presumably the filmmaker), her back to the viewing audience (we do not see her face), she is sitting, typing the words "Making Change 1936 Donkin, Nova Scotia", on a laptop computer. This scene cuts to a man (Conrad Coates) walking on a rural road wearing overalls and carrying a lunch pail. The piano is dominant among the instruments and a plodding rhythm is being played. The rural surroundings are lush, bright and green, and the man picks wild flowers before disappearing from the frame. When he next reappears, along with a faint melody, he has entered a small house and is seen presenting the flowers to his wife (Kala Perrin). The flowers are then carefully arranged in a vase on the dining table. The scene is in black and white and so is the remainder of the film, except for the last two minutes which return to colour. These shifts between colour and black and white, "silent movies", and the cinematic representation of jazz, is for me the filmmaker's attempt to "calibanize"[2] the various ways in which representations of black people have been organised and regulated in the history of the cinematic text, especially cinematic texts which work with jazz.

Philips's *Making Change* represents a new direction for black Canadian cinema because it skilfully and thoughtfully plays with the tensions of black Canadian representation while it simultaneously gestures to the interraciality of black Canadian historicity. The film is also a departure because it is not the kind of "neo-realist" narrative which seeks to document the realities of being black in a racist country. Despite seeming fictive, the film is autobiographical.[3] In fact, the way in which it's positioned circumscribes any discussion of racism with the traces and absences that the filmmaker leaves us to ponder, and not by explicit commentary in the film. What is also important about the film is the way in which it is both historical and contemporary. *Making Change* is both a film about black Canadian discontinuous histories and simultaneously a rendition of what those histories mean for the present. Philips's use of diasporic aesthetics are both cinematically conversant with a catalogue and archive of diasporic and Hollywood film making and intricately thought through in relation to her narrative.

Involved in representing "home" and its troubles, *Making Change* is a film concerned with what Quincy Troupe would call the "music of geography & place" (98), where black Canadians are cemented to the nation. The man, we learn, is a miner; and immediately images of death in the belly of the earth come to mind, speaking to the centrality of belonging in profound ways. This revelation makes black Canadians central to both the material and psychic structures of the nation, in spite of, and despite, official national denial.

But mining in the film also announces a plethora of issues, ones that have been relatively unexamined by black Canadian filmmakers. (Much of what I say here should be qualified by the work of black Canadian documentary filmmakers who have dedicated their time to uncovering the hidden histories of pre-modern and modern black life in Canada.) The cinematic rendering of a black Canadian modernity is evident. The camera, for example, lingers over the evidence of electricity, indoor plumbing, a sewing machine, photographs, a piano and a clock. For the first time in recent memory, a cinematic black Canadian "age of mechanical reproduction" is authored. The last scenes of the film show the man playing his clarinet: he's looking out over a coastal cliff, blowing a happy melody.

VI

The music of *Making Change* was composed by Michael Stuart (clarinet), Jonathan Goldsmith (piano) and David Nichol (guitar). They also play on the film's soundtrack. The man in the film is a clarinet player and composer who clearly desires to be a full-time musician.

Music is, therefore, a central component of *Making Change*; the "sight of music" (12), as Arthur Knight would put it, is everywhere. This visualizing of music that Philips's takes on is important for a number of reasons. One might be her engagement with a cinematic re-presentation of jazz. Further, music remains one of the most complex manifestations of diasporic aesthetic practices and, contrary to Michele Wallace's[4] claims concerning the lack of the visual in black cultures, it is a highly visible component of black cultures. Finally, the way in which Philips renders the role that women played in the support of male jazz musicians is notable. Here she questions the "macho" narratives of jazz as being totally outside the realm of "domesticity".

Let me begin with the last reason first. Once the man is at home, most of his time is spent composing music and playing. Moving between the piano, notation sheets, and the clarinet, the man tries to compose within the confines of the home. Immediately, Philips's place within the context of films concerning jazz becomes a signifying gesture. Jazz, like all art, is a studied practice, contrary to Theodore Adorno's[5] ill-informed claims concerning the genre. Jazz is not merely a spontaneous eruption from the black body. In fact, the man must negotiate the time and space needed for the act of creation between his small daughter's (Stephanie Brent) desire to play, and later his wife's sexual and sensual advances, which he gives into.

In this section of the film the music is light, soft and mellow. *Making Change* makes a strong case for uncovering the roles that domestic life and the accoutrements of modernity, including what the discourse of the housewife and black participation in that discourse, meant for the development of jazz as an art.[6] But the domesticity of the film also allows the audience to engage more closely with the man's desire to be a musician and to have some insight into his material and interior life. Shots of him running out of the house on more than one occasion, apparently late for work, contextualize his desire.

In a dream the man has after being given a poster by another man (Christian Service) driving a 1938 Dodge Brothers, he imagines himself playing his music in a club. He is dressed in a white tuxedo: the audience loves his music and applauds him wildly. His dream is countered by his wife's, who, on seeing the poster imagines herself as a Lady Day (Billie Holiday) lookalike with gardenia and all. In her dream there are no adoring crowds. Their dreams are important because they make interior desires evident. Her dream also pushes the ways in which Philips's diasporic aesthetics mark the film. Lady Day is clearly positioned as more than American — Lady Day becomes a diasporic icon recognizable and claimed by all who dare to do so. The absence of adoring crowds is therefore made ironic.

In another dream, the man has a vision of a pick-axe crashing into his table. After this dream he trashes the room where he composes. This dream propels him to act, and to attempt to achieve his desire. Awaking on the table the next day, he carefully packs his music and clarinet, and takes them to work in the mine where he plays as his co-workers, mainly white men, look on. One white miner even dances a jig. This makes the interraciality of jazz explicit and at the same time gestures to the racism of the Canadian mining industry. Miners were offered relatively well-paying jobs: but few went to blacks. The music at this point becomes much more upbeat and liberating. Towards the end of the film the suggestion seems to be that the man has given up working in the mine. He is shown strolling on a rural road, decked out in a hip urban style, with clarinet case, going somewhere. It looks like he is headed to a jam session. A melodious clarinet accompanies him.

Here, the music and the man's actions are in harmony. The use of music as voice in the film raises the question of visuality. Michele Wallace's claims concerning the privileging of music in black diasporic cultures vis-à-vis the visual is questioned by *Making Change*. The film clearly posits music as visual and the integration of music into the film as voice and subject matter alerts us to ways in which music brings with it a style, a language, and a syntax that demand visuality.

Making Change occupies a space which allows music to be one method for uncovering and opening up avenues for filling what Wallace calls "a visual void in black culture".[7] The sight of music in the film is both texture and textuality, which means the music is seen/scene.

Lastly, *Making Change* is in dialogue with a body of jazz films from *Cabin in the Sky* (1944) to 1996's *Kansas City* (made after *Making Change*). Jazz films like *Bird, Round Midnight, Mo' Better Blues* and many others have, to varying degrees, represented jazz as an art without breaking with stereotypes concerning black cinematic representations and general stereotypes concerning black expressive cultures. In *Making Change* there are no tensions between the sacred and secular; there is no sense of jazz as being decadent; drugs and alcohol are not a part of the man's on-screen life; he is not abusive to his wife and children. There is a small baby as well. In fact, in one scene accompanied by upbeat tempos, the man is seen flying a kite with his daughter and later rolling in the grass with her. *Making Change* engages with a history of cinematic representations of jazz and reworks those representations in a fashion that casts aside the mystery and intrigue usually attendant in these films.

The most important reworking in the film is the way in which the clarinet represents what Krin Gabbard, writing on representations of the trumpet in jazz films, calls a "post-phallic" (106) moment. The man's clarinet is not an extension of his life, it's a part of his life. The film is therefore not only richly intertextual, it's also a riffology, because of its intertextuality. Frederick Gaber has pointed out that jazz "is not solely immediate because it also owns a richly textured intertextual life, a life that, by any definition, finds itself at every point immersed in history" (91-92). Gaber's comments are important because they point to the ways in which

Making Change moves between various intertexts or significations which leave numerous traces or evidences for the audience to work with. The film's intertextuality and texture speaks to the histories it reworks and works over. The film re-presents cinematic jazz history as it immerses itself in black Canadian history and diasporic desire, pleasures, memories and disappointments. All these things are accomplished with subtlety and nuance, by worrying and troubling the lines of the (post)modern nation. The film is a doubled look at cinematic histories and national stories of belonging, and it repositions those histories and stories in a fashion not consumed by positive images but rather in a fashion that seeks to tentatively arrive at a grammar for thinking blackness in Canada.

VII

The last scene takes the filmmaker and audience into what Albert Murray would call "the blues territory" because Philips has the man play an upbeat, joyous tempo while walking towards a mountain-top or cliff which clearly looks out to the coast and ocean. Donkin, Nova Scotia, the locale for the film, is not only a rural mining town: it's also on the Cape Breton coast.

The absence of water, a symbol that has come to mark much aesthetically challenging black diasporic cinematic work (i.e. *Territories, Twilight City*) is reworked by Philips. She does not place water and its symbolic importance for diasporic blacks, however, on the screen: its importance is gestured to in other ways. There is an early frame of the man walking along the coast. The look or gaze out into the ocean is rather paradoxical because of the firmness with which the man is situated within the nation, on its soil. This "native son's" look or gaze outside is not representative of a desire to leave, like the maroons who were shipped to Africa via Nova

Scotia, or the black Nova Scotians who returned to Africa, to settle in Sierra Leone. The gaze could well be a symbolic welcoming of all the black migrants who will arrive in future years.

The gaze or look is a return of sorts to the past and at the same time a gesture to the present-future. It is a return in the form of the narrative of the film which documents a tiny aspect of black Canadian history. But this return is not stuck in the past. In fact, this return to the past is very much about the present-future because the opening shot, in colour, of a black woman writing "1936 Donkin Nova Scotia", coupled with the closing shot, also in colour, of the man joyously playing his clarinet, evokes a moment that speaks to the way in which the writer at the laptop is the (post)modern daughter who was once playful with her creative father as he attempted to compose music. Philips then is the symbolic and actual benefactor of the survival, resiliency, and creativity of a grammar of blackness which is clearly aware of the past, the present-future, and the tensions necessary for keeping them in play. *Making Change*, in its title and its cinematic site of music, its play with history and memory, and its locating of a black Canadian cinematic (post)modernity, requires us to make change in terms of how we construct cinematic representations of blackness in Canada. Philips's efforts take us down a long road: they begin to articulate a tentative and contingent grammar for black, one with its own Canadian syntaxes.

VIII

The project for black Canadian artists and critics is to articulate a grammar of black that is located within Canada's various regions, both urban and rural. The invention of a grammar for black in Canada that is aware of historical narrative and plays with that narrative is crucial in the struggle against erasure. A grammar for black needs to occupy a number of different kinds of positions, social and cultural identities, and political utterances. The articulation of a grammar for black, and ensuing contestations over it, is what will continue to imbibe the vital cultures of black Canadians with a continued dynamism. Critique, dialogues and conversations can move beyond the discourse of celebration to begin to account for the vitality of artistic expression, national and outer-national desires and disappointments, and a critical culture that is both honest and enabling. A grammar for black will take black Canadian cultures beyond the narrow and dreary confines of an anti-racism discourse, and allow us to concentrate on the various black selves in a fashion which enhances lives lived far beyond the clutches of racism. A grammar for black will cement blackness to the nation and reconfigure the nation for the better.

Endnotes

Chapter 1 "Going to the North"

1. By black Canadas I mean to signal the multiplicities of
black peoples in the geographic area called Canada and to
attend to the tensions of their differences. I assert the importance of this while fully aware of the ways in which nation-
state policies attempt to render those differences invisible
through a plethora of homogenizing practices. Yet this notion
of Canadas points to the ability of people to continue to exert
some measure of self-definition in the context of the nation-
state.

2. Paul Gilroy has already been called to task for the masculinist metaphor of the ship by Robert Reid-Pharr, and by
Norval Edwards for routes not taken. I agree with both Reid-
Pharr and Edwards. Therefore, I will not repeat those arguments here. Instead, 1 want to intervene in the cultural politics of ethnic absolutism or discreet social identities which are
currently being used to reorganise the academy, especially
when the talismanic word "diaspora" is appropriated and
manipulated by the context of national desire.

3. See Robin Winks, *The Blacks in Canada*; Daniel Hill, *The Freedom Seekers*.

4. See Robin Winks, *The Blacks in Canada*; Daniel Hill, *The Freedom Seekers*.

5. See the Miller introduction to *Blake*; also Gilroy, *The Black Atlantic*, chapter 1, for discussions of Delany's immigrationist tendencies.

6. Robin Winks, *The Blacks in Canada*; Daniel Hill, *The Freedom Seekers*; Peggy Bristow, et al., *'We're Rooted Here and They Can't Pull Us Up'*.

7. Peggy Bristow, et al., *'We're Rooted Here and They Can't Pull Us Up'*.

8. Manthia Diawara, "Black Studies, Cultural Studies"; Baker, *Black Studies, Rap and the Academy*. Both Diawara and Baker offer differing but complementary discussions of the relationship between black studies and black cultural studies. Their arguments could be construed as moving away from the centrality of black studies to black cultural studies.

9. See Peggy Bristow, "'Whatever you raise in the ground you can sell it in Chatham': Black women in Buxton and Chatham, 1850-65" in *'We're Rooted Here and They Can't Pull Us Up'*.

10. See *The Black Abolitionists' Papers*, in particular Delany's letter to Mary Ann Shadd for help in raising funds to buy some people out of slavery.

11. See Winks, *The Blacks in Canada*; Hill, *The Freedom-Seekers*; Bristow, et al, *'We're Rooted Here and They Can't Pull Us Up'*; Painter, "Martin R. Delany: Elitism and Black Nationalism"; Clarke, "A Primer of African-Canadian Literature".

12. See Peggy Bristow, *'We're Rooted Here and They Can't Pull Us Up'*.

13. This facility is located in North York, the city with

Canada's largest black population.

14. See Leslie Sanders, "American Script, Canadian Realities: Toronto's *Showboat*"; for further discussions of blackness, the Canadian nation-state, public institutions and public space see Eva Mackey, "Postmodernism and Cultural Politics in a Multicultural Nation: Contests over Truth in the *Into the Heart of Africa* Controversy"; and Rinaldo Walcott, "Lament for a Nation: The Racial Geography of 'The OH! Canada Project'".

15. The forces opposing the staging of *Showboat* brought in American John Henrik Clarke to counter the effects of Gates. I understand their practice as complicit with the notion that African-American commentary about the musical would be the important and authentic position. I think that this impeded their case as opposed to strengthening it or effectively countering Gates. This is one of those instances and situations where the limits and dangers of outer-national and transnational political identifications and actions are made evident — the disciplinary powers of the nation-state still remains intact for "citizens" who must be discredited.

16. In *Transition*, Selwyn Cudjoe's review of the work of M. Nourbese Philip found it wanting. While I agree with some of his criticisms re: Philip's last two collections of essays, his attack remains suspect. Let me elaborate. What is at stake in Cudjoe's review? What might be possible if he could acknowledge, or at least recognize the efficacy of local politics, polemics and interventions? And finally, what might be useful about understanding what I shall call both the place and space of blackness in Canada? Would it help to make sense of Philip's local interventions? Cudjoe argues that Philip makes crude generalizations and correlations between art (the musical *Showboat*) and racism, which in turn is evidence of her inability to understand the dynamics of art and

racism. What Cudjoe appears incapable of doing is addressing the specificities of localized black Canadian politics, because his knowledge of both art and racism in Canada seems rather shallow. Instead, he reads Philip's intervention through the lens of the United States.

17. These questions are informed by Hazel Carby's *Reconstructing Womanhood*, in particular the tough questions she poses for (black) feminism. She writes: "What I want to advocate is that black feminist criticism be regarded *critically as a problem*, not a solution, as a sign that should be interrogated, *a locus of contradictions*" (15, emphasis added). I too believe that black studies and black diasporic theorizing need to be considered signs of, and a locus for, interrogation.

18. While I think that it is historically correct and politically astute to argue for *The Souls of Black Folk* as the founding text of black studies and black cultural studies, the conceptual question of genealogical positioning is never complete. How do we place Marcus Garvey's equally important insights into this debate (surely DuBois had to write against some of them); C.L.R. James should also be accounted for; while Stokely Carmichael (Kwame Toure), and his involvement in the civil rights and black power era, points to the place of the Caribbean in the seminal battles of black studies; these issues are important because they illustrate the antinomies of diasporic theorizing.

19. See for example Stella Algoo-Baksh's biography of Austin Clarke, in particular the chapter "Into Academia" (78-104), for the role that Clarke played in black studies programs and politics from the late 1960s to the 1970s at Yale, Brandeis, Duke and the University of Texas at Austin. This is just one peregrination that might open up other ways of thinking through black studies and the flight to black cultural studies by some scholars.

20. See the recent article "Black Like Them" in the *Blacks in America* special issue of *The New Yorker* — written by a Canadian.

21. It is important to note that the Canadian relay team all had roots/routes to many places, and Canada was only one among a number of others — the Caribbean played a prominent role in the team's biographies. Their own tangential relationship to the Canadian nation-state was made evident when a national debate ensued because Donovan Bailey was quoted as stating that little difference existed between the United States and Canada when it came to the practice of racism.

22. *The Globe and Mail,* September 19, 1996; also see Leavy, "Blacks and The Biggest Olympics" in *Ebony* for a pictorial essay demonstrating the skilful burial of the black Canadian presence and accomplishments. Bailey's photo comes near the end, while Johnson's photo opens the series; the Canadian relay team is not pictured at all.

23. See Robin Winks, *The Blacks in Canada*; Daniel Hill, *The Freedom-Seekers* .

24. See Tricia Rose, *Black Noise: Rap Music and Black Culture in Contemporary America,* in which she uses the talisman "Afrodiasporic" to signal the borrowing and exchanges of rap music but does not follow up the implications of diaspora in her discussion. Instead she reads rap entirely within the discourse of a nation — the United States. For a counter to Rose, see Juan Flores's "Puerto Rican and Proud, Boyee!: Rap Roots and Amnesia" where he argues for reading Puerto Rican contributions to hip-hop histories; and George Lipsitz in *Dangerous Crossroads* for a transnational and multicultural reading of rap and other dissident popular musical genres.

Chapter 2 "A Tough Geography"

1. This essay is an amalgam of ideas which I believe need to be given more attention in approaches to black Canadian literature. In many instances scholars writing on black Canadian literature have been reluctant to address what the literature means for "here" and instead read the works entirely within an outsider discourse. I wish to thank Leslie Sanders for her helpful suggestions.

2. Winks, *Blacks In Canada: A History*; Clarke, *Fire on the Water: An Anthology of Black Nova Scotian Writing Vol. 1*; Bristow et al, *'We're Rooted Here and They Can't Pull Us Up'*.

3. See Walcott, "Lament for A Nation: The Racial Geography of 'The Oh! Canada Project'".

4. Clarke, *Fire on the Water: An Anthology of Black Nova Scotian Writing Vol. 2*.

5. *Fire on the Water Vol. 1*.

6. Clarke, "A Primer of African-Canadian Literature".

7. *And Now The Legacy Begins...*

8. Foster also tackles the issue of reunification and its not so pleasant side in *Sleep On Beloved*, but I believe that a fundamental difference exists in the way Brand covers this painful territory by extricating it from the realm of the individual to address questions of collective responsibility.

Chapter 3 The Politics of Third Cinema in Canada

1. Snead, *White Screens, Black Images: Hollywood from the Dark Side*.

2. Gabriel, "Towards a Critical Theory of Third World Films"; for a broad discussion of third cinema see *Black Frames: Critical Perspectives on Black Independent Cinema*, M.

Cham and C. Andrade-Watkins (eds.); *Questions of Third Cinema*, J. Pines and P. Willemen (eds.); *Ex-Iles: Essays on Caribbean Cinema*, M. Cham (ed.).

3. See chapter six.

4. Glassman, "Where Zulus Meet Mohawks: Clement Virgo's *Rude*".

5. "Filling the lack in everyone is quite hard work, really..." A roundtable discussion with Joy Chamberlain, Isaac Julien, Stuart Marshall, and Pratibha Parmar; Rich, B. Ruby, "When Difference Is (More Than) Skin Deep".

6. Britzman, "Decentring Discourses in Teacher Education: Or, the Unleashing of Unpopular Things".

Chapter 4 "Keep on Movin'"

1. *Capitalism & Schizophrenia: A Thousand Plateaus*.

2. Gilroy, "Cultural Studies and Ethnic Absolutism." Gilroy first used the term black Atlantic in this essay as a way of making sense of black cultural and political exchanges and to resist ethnic absolutist claims concerning black intellectual contributions. See *Black Atlantic: Modernity and Double Consciousness*. The black Atlantic is developed conceptually and theoretically as an expansive space that traverses time, history, memory and the workings of black, and in particular black metropolitan, communities' cultural practices. I use the term after Gilroy to reference the importance of black diasporic cultures, practices of exchange, and dialogues, and how those patterns might structure local politics and trans-national politics. I do not use black Atlantic as a way to essentialize blackness across space and time.

3. Edward Kamau Brathwaite, "The African Presence in Caribbean Literature". Brathwaite argues and demonstrates

through a reading of Paula Marshall's *Praisesong for the Widow* that African elements in Caribbean literature are important moments of not only acknowledgement of an African past but of a desire and a practice of what he calls reconnection. I think that Brathwaite's insight can be usefully extended to other syncretic, artistic "new world" black practices like film, fine art, dance and music.

4. Clearly, Palestinian claims to parts of the territory of Israel complicate the question of Israel as a nation-state. However, without denying that important history I am attempting to gesture to the fluidity of the origins of the Israeli nation-state and to address some of the contemporary "problems" that have accompanied claims to the nation-state outside of Palestinian demands.

5. *Imagined Communities: Reflections on the Origin and Spread of Nationalism.*

6. ibid.

7. "Introduction: Narrating the Nation". *Nation and Narration.*

8. *The Nation and Its Fragments: Colonial and Postcolonial Histories.*

9. I borrow this term from Roxana Ng, "Multiculturalism as Ideology: A Textual Accomplishment".

10. Canadian Multicultural Act. Federal Multicultural Policy.

11. *Selling Illusions: The Cult of Multiculturalism in Canada.* This is the Canadian equivalent to the American conservative cultural agenda. While Bissoondath's critique of multiculturalism is generally warranted, he too is tied to notions of Canada and thus nation as fundamentally dualistic. He can perceive of no way beyond the dichotomous bind other than to suggest taking on either the "culture" of Quebec or Anglo Canadians. He believes the former has a more secure sense of

self and is thus exemplary. His approach harkens back to the modernist nation-state narrative of one unified people when he argues that only Quebecers know their culture and thus they should be the model that is used to renew Canada as a viable nation-state. Such assertions seem to advocate a cultural imperialism of the worst kind, one which has been generally applauded by the mainstream media.

12. For an extensive discussion of these institutions see M. Nourbese Philip, "The 'Multicultural' Whitewash: Racism in Ontario's Art Funding System".

13. *Oral/Trans/Missions.*

14. I use "signifyin" here in the way that H.L. Gates Jr., in *The Signifying Monkey: A Theory of African-American Literary Criticism*, uses it: to denote the African-American practice or black diasporic practices of double-voicing, revision of dominant meanings, and other ways of inverting meaning so as to not only act as a form of resistance but to also pass on information that only those intimate with the culture or those who are subtle cultural readers might understand.

15. Snead, "Repetition as a Figure of Black Culture."

16. *Playing in the Dark: Whiteness and the Literary Imagination.*

17. Boyce-Davies, *Black Women, Writing and Identity: Migrations of the Subject.* Boyce-Davies engages in a theoretical discussion of the "elsewhereness" of diasporic sensibilities as important to black women's writing and black cultural politics in general.

18. *Revolutionary Tea Party. Women, Do This Everyday: Selected Poems of Lillian Allen.* In the preface to her selected poems Allen writes of having to "finalize" poems for the page, poems she had never thought of as final. The process of finalization evokes the tensions between the oral and the written and the performativity of both in her work.

19. See Dionne Brand's numerous collections of poetry; in particular *No Language is Neutral* and *Winter Epigrams & Epigrams To Ernesto Cardenal In Defence of Claudia*. On Maestro Fresh-Wes's most recent album his hypercommentary on Canada, the track titled "Certs Wid Out Da Retsyn", might be read as Canada's attempt to deny colour at its centre; the Dream Warriors, on their first album *And Now the Legacy Begins* have a track titled "Ludi" in which they name almost every Caribbean island as well as Canadian localities as an indication of who and what they are.

20. "The African World and The Ethnocultural Debate". I want to suggest that some articulations of Afrocentrism produce the pastoral romantic Africa or the Africa of kings and queens; some of the work that I am discussing is not immune from such discourses but I have focused on the fluid tracks as a way of demonstrating what I believe to be the undeniable relations of diasporic groups.

21. Capitol Records-EMI of Canada.

22. Sharrif, "Highrise Divide" and "Somali dust-up with guards sparks riot". A television documentary on the Dixon Road controversy aired on *The Journal* on the CBC. Some of my information is based on that documentary.

24. ibid.

25. Saenger, "Somalia's Welfare Warlords". The author of the article is at great pains to point out how widespread welfare fraud is among Somalis but is only able to offer evidence of two convictions. Saenger then proceeds to implicate Nigerian immigrants in past welfare fraud but produces no evidence. Much of the article is concerned with locating exactly where Somalis are living in Canada, almost as if to suggest that they need not be here at all.

26. I use "blackening" here to point to a process or practice of racialization. Important, however, are the ways in which

that process might be performed by those who are at once named as black and at the same time use it as the basis of their counterhegemonic discourse. J. Butler *(Bodies that Matter: On the Discursive Limits of "Sex".)* suggests that the ways in which performativity works is that it puts a discourse into practice. Thus blackness/black as categories only become intelligible when the discourses that constitute them are acted out either as relations of subordination or as practices of (re)fashioning the self.

27. "DissemiNation: Time, Narrative and the Margins of the Modern Nation".

28. The epistemology of racism runs deep in the battle. The introduction of dogs into the picture draws heavily on racialized imagery of black peoples' supposed fear of dogs. Islamic practices concerning dogs, and in particular dog bites, can cause great trauma for any "good" practicing Muslim, and this complicates things further. The owners insist on employing guards with dogs despite a task force report recommendation that suggested the guard force itself was unnecessary since no major crime problem exists. In fact, crime apparently decreased when the Somalis arrived. In the most recent battle, the underlying sexual stereotype of agressive black males has surfaced: white neighbours claim that they cannot send their daughters for groceries because "youth" (read black males) are hanging around outside the store.

29. In the CBC documentary the camera idles for quite some time on the T-shirt of one outspoken youth. The significance of his T-shirt is that the words "Malcolm X" adorn the front.

30. Sharrif, "Highrise Divide".

31. *Talkin and Testifyin: The Language of Black America.*

32. *Post-National Arguments: The Politics of the Anglophone-Canadian Novel Since 1967.*

33. *Splitting Images: Contemporary Canadian Ironies.*
34. ibid.

Chapter 5 "No Language is Neutral"

1. *The Writing of History.*
2. "Twentieth-Century Fiction and the Black Mask of Humanity".
3. "Discourse on the Logic of Language".
4. "No Language is Neutral".
5. Mackey, "Other From Noun to Verb".
6. Gates, "Introduction: Writing 'race' and the difference it makes"; Walcott, "'Out of the Kumbla': Toni Morrison's Jazz and Pedagogical Answerability".
7. Bannerji, "The Poetry of Dionne Brand"; Goddard, "Marlene Nourbese Philip's Hyphenated Tongue or Writing the Caribbean Demotic between Africa and Arctic"; Sarbadhikary, "Weaving a 'Multicoloured Quilt': Marlene Nourbese Philip's Vision of Change"; Case, "Poetic Discourse in Babylon: The Poetry of Dionne Brand".
8. Abrahams, *Singing the Master: The Emergence of African-American Culture in the Plantation South.* In this study Abrahams addresses the various ways in which slaves in the Americas invented identities and discarded them as forms of resistance and survival in plantation societies.
9. In both Philip's and Brand's poetry photography is central to at least one poem. But what is even more interesting is how they use photography to jog the memory and how they read photographs as a woman's way of conveying information in tension with the writing of women's personal and collective histories. See the poems "The Catechist" (Philip) and "Blues Spiritual for Mammy Prater" (Brand).

10. Gates, *The Signifying Monkey: A Theory of African-American Literary Criticism*; Gates argues that one of the practices of African-American signifying is textual revision. Mackey has clearly revised Jones.

11. Henderson, "Speaking in Tongues: Dialogics, Dialectics and the Black Women Writers' Literary Tradition", 138.

12. Godard, "Marlene Nourbese Philip's Hyphenated Tongue or Writing the Caribbean Demotic between Africa and Arctic".

13. Nancy, *The Inoperative Community*; see the discussions on "community as sacred."

14. *History of the Voice: The Development of Nation Language in Anglophone Caribbean Poetry*.

15. See Cooper, "'Something ancestral recaptured': spirit possession as trope in selected feminist fictions of the African diaspora"; Foucault, *Power/Knowledge: Selected Interviews & Other Writings 1972-1977*.

16. *Out of the Kumbla: Caribbean Women and Literature*.

17. Soloman-Godeau, "Mistaken Identities". In this catalogue essay, Solomon-Godeau argues that the strategies used by marginalized artists do not merely invert and reverse, they shift and alter the ways of knowing and making sense and in many cases unsettle presumptions concerning identities leading to mistaken identities. I think her ideas are useful for thinking about Philip's and Brand's poetic works.

18. Bakhtin, *Speech Genres & Other Late Essays*, 60.

19. Smitherman, *Talkin and Testifyin: The Language of Black America*, 1-15; Brathwaite, *History of the Voice: The Development of Nation Language in Anglophone Caribbean Poetry*.

20. See either the recorded music/poetry or books of Lillian Allen, Ahdri Zhina Mandiela and Clifton Joseph.

21. Fusco, "Managing the Other". Fusco argues that all these things have been a vital part of the colonized cultural practice because it was the only way that they could survive the atrocities of colonialism. Hybridity, in this sense, becomes a useful and important part of resistance. Contemporary valorization of these practices often pays little attention to colonized histories, the long and varied use of bricolage, indirection, reversal and so on, and thus many "post-colonial" subjects remain sceptical of postmodernist discourse.

22. Mackey uses the term calibanization, drawing on Brathwaite's *Mother Poem*.

23. See Durham, "Cowboys and..."; Morrison, *Playing in the Dark: Whiteness and the Literary Imagination*.

24. *Splitting Images: Contemporary Canadian Ironies*.

25. For readings of Caribbean poetry that take history and place into careful consideration, as well as language and the rewriting of dominant ways of knowing, see J.E. Chamberlin, *Come Back To Me My Language: Poetry and the West Indies*.

26. Brathwaite, *History of the Voice: The Development of Nation Language in Anglophone Caribbean Poetry*; see in particular section 8.

27. Boyce-Davies, "Introduction: Migratory Subjectivities: Black Women's Writing and the Re-negotiation of Identities". In the essay Boyce-Davies plots the travels of her mother as a symbolic, actual and metaphorical indication of a travelling history/memory and fluid community. What Boyce-Davies uses her mother's travels to demonstrate is the ways in which crossing borders for black migratory subjects is always an act that invokes community through various moments of identification.

28. *The Writing of History*.

29. See the essay "The African Presence in Caribbean

Literature" in *Roots*; in this essay Brathwaite provides a reading of Paula Marshall's *Praisesong for the Widow*, which he argues is a text of reconnection.

Chapter 6 Black Subjectivities

1. Philip, "How White is Your White?: On The Lack of Colour in the Bernardo/Homolka Affair".

2. Sophia Cook (paralyzed), Michael Wade Lawson, Royan Bagnaut, Albert Johnson, Buddy Evans, Michael Sargeant, Raymond Lawrence, Johnathan Howell and Tommy Barnett.

3. See Diawara, "Black American Cinema: The New Realism".

4. See Bailey, "A Cinema of Duty: The Films of Jennifer Hodge De Silva". Bailey argues that black Canadian cinema is characterized by the documentary influences of the National Film Board and state funding. De Silva's films were all documentaries with some intent of rewriting stereotypes or representing the authentic black person in Canada. While Williams's and Virgo's films are not documentaries the underlying premises draw on a realist narrative of what it might mean to be black in Canada.

5. Williams made one other short film prior to his feature called *Variation on a Key 2 Life* (30 min.). Virgo made two short films, *Small Dick Fleshy Ass Thing* and *Save My Lost Nigga' Soul*.

6. Walcott, "'Voyage Through the Multiverse': Contested Canadian Identities"; I argue that multicultural policy in Canada works to simultaneously narrate how blackness might be imagined as Canadian and to render blackness outside the nation through the discourse of heritage.

7. See Marc Glassman and Angela Baldassarre, both in *Take One*.

8. Walcott, R.

9. See Nazareth, "Training use of Boyz gets blacks' thumbs-down." *Now Magazine*, August 15-21: 19.

10. See Watts: 22.

11. For more on Esu see Henry Louis Gates Jr., *The Signifying Monkey: A Theory of African-American Literary Criticism*.

12. See Butler; for Diawara identity is produced through complex and shifting identifications that are made though the complex process of how we respond individually and collectively to various discourses.

13. A similar theme exists in *Variation* when Cherry O'Baby decides to leave the protagonist Skill Blackstock.

14. See M. Nourbese Philip, *Frontiers: Essays and Writings on Racism and Culture*. See, in that collection, the "Introduction" and "The 'Multicultural' Whitewash: Racism in the Ontario Art Funding System".

Chapter 7 Scattered Speculations on Canadian Blackness

1. Leslie Sanders, "American Script, Canadian Realities: Toronto's *Showboat*".

2. Nathaniel Mackey, "Other: From Noun to Verb".

3. Leslie Sanders, "Anti/Modern Spaces: African Canadians in Nova Scotia".

4. "Afterword: 'Why Are There No Great Black Artists?' The Problem of Visuality in African-American Culture" and "Modernism, Postmodernism and the Problem of the Visual in Afro-American Culture".

5. "Perrenial Fashion-Jazz".

6. Elsa Barkley Brown, "Negotiating and Transforming the Public Sphere: African American Political Life in the

Transition from Slavery to Freedom".

7. Wallace, "AfterWord: 'Why Are There No Great Black Artists?' The Problem of Visuality in African-American Culture", 344.

Selected Bibliography

Abrahams, R.D. *Singing the Master: The Emergence of African-American Culture in The Plantation South.* New York: Penguin Books, 1992.

Adorno, T. W. "Perennial Fashion-Jazz". *Prisms.* Trans. S. and S. Weber. Cambridge, MA: MIT Press, 1982.

Algoo-Baksh, S. *Austin Clarke: A Biography.* Toronto: ECW Press and The Press of the University of the West Indies, 1994.

Allen, L. *Women Do This Everyday: Selected Poems of Lillian Allen.* Toronto: Women's Press, 1993.

Anderson, B. *Imagined Communities: Reflections on the Origin and Spread of Nationalism.* London: Verso, 1983.

Bailey, C. "A Cinema of Duty: The Films of Jennifer Hodge De Silva". *CineAction 23* (Winter, 1990-91): 4-12.

Baker, H., Jr. *Black Studies, Rap and the Academy.* Chicago: University of Chicago Press, 1993.

Bakhtin, M. *Speech Genres and Other Late Essays.* Trans. V.W. McGee. Austin, TX: University of Texas Press, 1986.

———. *Art and Answerability: Early Philosophical Essays.* Trans. V. Liapunov. Ed. M. Holquist and V. Liapunov. Austin, TX: University of Texas Press, 1990.

Bannerji, H. "The Poetry of Dionne Brand". *The Writing on the Wall: Essays on Culture and Politics.* Toronto: TSAR, 1993.

Banning, K. "Rhetorical Remarks Towards The Politics of Otherness". *CineAction 16* (Spring, 1989): 14-19.

Baldassarre, A. "Stephen Williams: *Soul Survivor*". *Take One* Vol.4, No.9, (1995): 32-35.

Bhabha, H. "Introduction: Narrating the Nation". "DissemiNation: Time, Narrative and the Margins of the Modern Nation". *Nation and Narration.* Ed. H. Bhabha. London: Routledge, 1990.

Bissoondath, N. *Selling Illusions: The Cult of Multiculturalism in Canada.* Toronto: Penguin Books, 1994.

Boyce-Davies, C. *Black Women, Writing and Identity: Migrations of the Subject.* New York: Routledge, 1994.

Brand, D. *Sans Souci and Other Stories.* Toronto: Williams-Wallace, 1988.

———. *No Language is Neutral.* Toronto: Coach House, 1990.

———. *Bread Out of Stone: Recollections, Sex, Recognitions, Race, Dreaming, Politics.* Toronto: Coach House, 1994.

———. *In Another Place Not Here.* Toronto: Alfred A. Knopf Canada, 1996.

Brathwaite, K. (1993). *Roots.* Ann Arbor, MI: University of Michigan Press, 1993.

———. *History of the Voice: The Development of Nation Language in Anglophone Caribbean Poetry.* London: New Beacon Books, 1984.

———. "The Love Axe/1,2,3:(Developing a Caribbean Aesthetic 1962-1974)". *Bim* (1975): 53-192.

Bristow, P., et al. *"We're Rooted Here and They Can't Pull Us Up": Essays in African-Canadian Women's History.* Toronto: University of Toronto Press, 1994.

Brown, E. "Negotiating and Transforming the Public Sphere: African-American Political Life in the Transition from Slavery to Freedom". *Public Culture* Vol.7, No.1 (Fall, 1994): 107-146.

Britzman, D. "Decentering Discourses in Teacher Education: Or, the Unleashing of Unpopular Things". *Boston University Journal of Education* Vol.173, No.3, (1991): 60-80.

Butler, J. *Bodies That Matter: On the Discursive Limits of "Sex".* New York: Routledge, 1993.

———. *Gender Trouble: Feminism and the Subversion of Identity.* New York: Routledge, 1990.

Canadian Multicultural Act. House of Commons Canada, 1988.

Carby, H. *Reconstructing Womanhood: The Emergence of the Afro-American Woman Novelist.* New York: Oxford University Press, 1987.

Case, F.I. "Poetic Discourse in Babylon: The Poetry of Dionne

Brand". *The Reordering of Culture: Latin America, The Caribbean and Canada, In the Hood.* Ed. A. Ruprecht and C. Taiana. Ottawa: Carleton University Press, 1995.

Cham, M., Andrade-Watkins, C. Ed. *Blackframes: Critical Perspectives on Black Independent Cinema.* Cambridge: MIT Press, 1988.

Cham, M. Ed. *Ex-Iles: Essays on Caribbean Cinema.* Trenton, NJ: African World Press Inc., 1992.

Chamberlain, J., I. Julien, S. Marshall, P. Parmar. "Filling the lack in everyone is quite hard work, really...". *Queer Looks: Perspectives on Lesbian and Gay Film and Video.* Ed. M. Gever, P. Parmar and J. Greyson. Toronto: Between the Lines, 1993.

Chamberlin, J.E. *Come Back to Me My Language: Poetry and the West Indies.* Toronto: McClelland and Stewart Inc., 1993.

Chatterjee, P. *The Nation and Its Fragments: Colonial and Postcolonial Histories.* Princeton, NJ: Princeton University Press, 1993.

Christie, J. "Bailey returns in triumph". *The Globe and Mail* (September, 1996): E16.

Clarke, G.E., Ed. *Fire on the Water: An Anthology of Black Nova Scotian Writing Vol.1.* Nova Scotia: Pottersfield Press, 1991.

———. Ed. *Fire on the Water: An Anthology of Black Nova Scotian Writing Vol.2.* Nova Scotia: Potterfield Press, 1992.

———. "A Primer of African-Canadian Literature". *Books in Canada* Vol.25, No.2 (March, 1996): 7-9.

Cooper, C. "'something ancestral recaptured': spirit possession as trope in selected feminist fictions of the African diaspora". *Motherlands: Black Women's Writing from Africa, the Caribbean and South Asia.* Ed. S. Nasta. London: The Women's Press, 1991.

Cudjoe, S. R. "Disturbing the Peace: The Scourge of Literary Canada Sacrifices Subtlety for Substance". *Transition 63* (1994): 51-58.

Davey, F. *Post-National Arguments: The Politics of the Anglophone-*

    Canadian Novel Since 1967. Toronto: University of Toronto
    Press, 1993.

De Certeau, M. *The Writing of History*. Trans. T. Conley. New
    York: Columbia University Press, 1988.

Delany, M. R. *The Condition, Elevation, Emigration, and Destiny of the
    Colored People of the United States*. New York: Arno Press
    and the New York Times, 1968.

————. *Blake; Or the Huts of America*. Boston: Beacon Press, 1970.

Deleuze, G. and F. Guattari, (1987). *Capitalism & Schizophrenia: A
    Thousand Plateaus*. Trans. B. Massumi. Minneapolis:
    University of Minnesota, 1987.

Diawara, M. "Black Studies, Cultural Studies, Performative Acts".
    Border/lines 29/30 (1993): 21-26.

————. "Black American Cinema: The New Realism". *Black
    American Cinema*. Ed. M. Diawara. New York: Routledge, 1993.

Durham, J. "Cowboys and..." *Third Text* No.12, (Autumn, 1990): 5-20.

Edwards, N. "Roots, and some Routes not Taken: A Caribcentric
    Reading of The Black Atlantic". *Found Object* 4 (Fall,1994):
    27-35.

Ellison, R. "Twentieth-Century Fiction and the Black Mask of
    Humanity". *Shadow and Act*. New York: Vintage
    International, 1995.

Fanon, F. *Black Skin White Mask*. Trans. L. Markman. New York:
    Grove Press, 1967.

Federal Multicultural Policy. House of Commons, Canada, 1971.

Flores, J. "Puerto Rican and Proud Boyee!: Rap Roots and
    Amnesia". *Microphone Fiends: Youth Music and Youth
    Culture*. Ed. A. Ross and T. Rose. New York: Routledge,
    1994.

Foster, C. *No Man in the House*. Toronto: Vintage Books, 1991.

————. *Sleep On Beloved*. Toronto: Random House, 1995.

Foucault, M. *Power/Knowledge: Selected Interviews & Other Writings
    1972-1977*. Ed. C. Gordon. New York: Pantheon Books, 1980.

————. *The History of Sexuality: An Introduction, Vol. 1.* Trans. R. Hurley. New York: Vintage, 1980.

Freud, S. *Civilization and Its Discontents.* Trans. J. Strachey. New York: W.W. Norton & Company, 1961.

Fusco, C. "Managing the Other". *Lusitania* Vol.1, No.3, (Fall,1990): 77-83.

Gabbard, K. "Signifyin(g) the Phallus: Mo' Better Blues and Representations of the Jazz Trumpet". *Representing Jazz.* Ed. K. Gabbard. Durham, NC: Duke University Press, 1995.

Gabriel, T. "Towards a Critical Theory of Third World Films". *Questions of Third Cinema.* Ed. J. Pines and P. Willemen. London: British Film Institute, 1989.

Gates, H.L. *The Signifying Monkey: A Theory of African-American Criticism.* Cambridge: Oxford University Press, 1988.

————. "Introduction: Writing 'Race' and the Difference It Makes". *"Race," Writing, and Difference.* Ed. H.L. Gates Jr.. Chicago: University of Chicago Press, 1985.

Gilroy, P. "Cultural Studies and Ethnic Absolutism". *Cultural Studies.* Ed. Lawrence Grossberg, et al. New York: Routledge, 1992.

————. *The Black Atlantic: Modernity and Double Consciousness.* Cambridge: Harvard University Press, 1993.

Gladwell, M. "Black Like Them". *The New Yorker*, April 29 & May 6, (1996): 74-81.

Glassman, M. "Where Zulus Meet Mohawks: Clement Virgo's Rude". *Take One* Vol.4, No.9, (1995): 17-21.

Glissant, E. *Caribbean Discourse: Selected Essays.* Trans. J.M. Dash. Charlottesville, VA: University Press of Virginia, 1989.

Godard, B. "Marlene Nourbese Philip's Hyphenated Tongue or Writing the Caribbean Demotic between Africa and Arctic". *Major Minorities: English Literatures in Transit.* Ed. R. Granqvist. Amsterdam: Ropodi, 1993.

Goldberg, T. D. *Racist Culture: Philosophy and the Politics of Meaning.*
Oxford: Blackwell, 1993.

Hall, S. "Cultural Identity and Cinematic Representation". *Ex-Iles:
Essays on Caribbean Cinema.* Ed. M. Cham. Trenton, NJ:
Africa World Press, Inc., 1992.

———. "What is This 'Black' in Black Popular Culture?" *Black
Popular Culture.* Ed. G. Dent. Seattle: Bay Press, 1992.

Harris, C. *Dipped in Shadows.* Fredericton, NB: Goose Lane
Editions, 1996.

Harris, W. "In the Name of Liberty". *Third Text* No.11,
(Summer, 1990): 7-15.

Henderson G.M. "'Where, by the way, is this train going?': A Case
for Black (Cultural) Studies". *Callaloo* Vol.19, No.1 (1996) 60-67.

Henderson, G.M. "Speaking in Tongues: Dialogics, Dialectics and
the Black Women Writers' Literary Tradition". *Changing
Our Own Words: Essays on Criticism, Theory, and Writing by
Black Women.* Ed. C. Wall. New Brunswick, NJ: Rutgers
University Press, 1989.

———. "Toni Morrison's Beloved: re-membering the body as
historical text". *Comparative American Identities: Race, Sex
and Nationality in the Modern Text.* Ed. H. Spillers. New
York: Routledge, 1991.

Hill, D. *The Freedom-Seekers: Blacks in Early Canada.* Agincourt, ON:
The Books Society of Canada Limited, 1981.

Hutcheon, L. *Splitting Images: Contemporary Canadian Ironies.*
Toronto: Oxford University Press, 1991.

James, C.L.R. *American Civilisation.* London: Blackwell, 1993.

Jones, L. *Blues People: The Negro Experience in White America and the Music
that Developed From It.* New York: Morrow Quilt Paperbacks,
1963.

Knight, A. "Jammin' the Blues, or the Sight of Jazz, 1944".
Representing Jazz. Ed. K Gabbard. Durham, NC: Duke
University Press, 1995.

Leavy, W. "Blacks and The Biggest Olympics". *Ebony*
    (October, 1996): 112-146.

Lipsitz, G. *Dangerous Crossroads: Popular Muisc, Postmodernism and the
    Poetics of Place*. London: Verso, 1994.

Lubiano, W. "Mapping the Interstices Between Afro-American
    Cultural Discourse and Cultural Studies: A
    Prolegomenon". *Callaloo* Vol.19, No.1 (1996): 68-77.

Mackey, E. "Postmodernism and Cultural Politics in a Multicultural
    Nation: Contests over Truth in the *Into the Heart of
    Africa* Controversy". *Public Culture* Vol.7, No.2 (Winter,
    1995): 403-431.

Mackey, N. "Other: From Noun to Verb". *Jazz Among the Discourses*.
    Ed. K. Gabbard. Durham, NC: Duke University Press, 1995.

Mannete, J. *Setting The Record Straight: The Experiences of Black People in
    Nova Scotia, 1780-1900*. Masters Thesis. Carleton University,
    1983.

McTair, R. ed. *The Black Experience in the White Mind: Mediations on
    a Persistent Discourse*. Toronto: PP, 1995.

Morrison, T. *Playing in the Dark: Whiteness and the Literary
    Imagination*. Cambridge, MA: Harvard University Press, 1992.

Murray, A. *The Blue Devils of Nada*. New York: Pantheon, 1996.

Nancy, J. *The Inoperative Community*. Trans. P. Connor, L. Garbus,
    M. Holland and S. Sawhney. Minneapolis: University of
    Minnesota Press, 1991.

Ng, R. "Multiculturalism as Ideology: A Textual Accomplishment".
    Paper presented at the 91st Annual Meeting of the
    American Anthropological Association, San Francisco,
    CA, 1992.

Parker, A. and E.K. Sedgwick, "Introduction: Performativity and
    Performance". *Performativity and Performance*. Ed. A.
    Parker and E.K. Sedgwick. New York: Routledge, 1995.

Philip, M.N. *Frontiers: Essays and Writings on Racism and Culture*.
    Stratford, ON: The Mercury Press, 1992.

———. "How White is Your White?: On The Lack of Colour in the Bernardo/Homolka Affair". *Border/lines* 38/39, (1995): 6-13.

———. *She Tries Her Tongue Her Silence Softly Breaks.* Charlottetown, P.E.I.: Ragweed Press, 1989.

Pianter, N. "Martin R. Delany: Elitism and Black Nationalism". *Black Leaders of the Nineteenth Century.* Ed. L. Litwack and A. Meier. Urbana, IL: University of Illinois Press, 1988.

Reed, I. *Flight to Canada.* New York: Athenuem, 1989.

Reid-Pharr, R.F. "Engendering the Black Atlantic". *Found Object*, Issue 4, (Fall, 1994): 11-16.

———. "Violent Ambiguity: Martin Delany, Bourgeois Sadomasochism, and the Production of a Black National Masculinity". *Representing Black Men.* Ed. M. Blount and G.P. Cunningham. New York: Routledge, 1996.

Ripley, P. Ed. *The Black Abolitionists' Papers, Vol.11, Canada, 1830-1865.* Chapel Hill, NC: The University of North Carolina Press, 1986.

Rose, T. *Black Noise: Rap Music and Black Culture in Contemporary America.* Hanover: Wesleyan University Press, 1994.

Saenger, E. "Somalia's Welfare Warlords". *Western Report* November 8th, (1993).

Sanders, L. "American Script, Canadian Realities: Toronto's Showboat". *Diaspora* Vol.5, No.1 (Spring, 1996): 99-118.

———. "Anti/Modern Spaces: African Canadians in Nova Scotia". Unpublished Manuscript, York University, Canada.

Sarbadhikary, K. (1994). "Weaving a "Multicoloured Quilt": Marlene Nourbese Philip's Vision of Change". *International Journal of Canadian Studies* 10, (Fall, 1994): 103-118.

Sharrif, A. "Highrise Divide". Toronto, *Now Magazine* (1993).

———. "Somali dust-up with guards sparks riot". *Now Magazine* (1994).

Smitherman, G. *Talkin and Testifyin: The Language of Black America.* Detroit: Wayne State University, 1977.

Snead, J. *White Screens, Black Images: Hollywood from the Dark Side.* New York: Routledge, 1994.

———. "Repetition as a Figure of Black Culture". *Out There: Marginalization and Contemporary Cultures.* Ed. R. Ferguson, M. Gever, T. Minh-ha and C. West. New York: The New Museum of Contemporary Art and The MIT Press, 1990.

Soloman-Godeau, A. "Mistaken Identities". *Mistaken Identities Catalogue.* California: The Regents of the University of California, 1993.

Soyinka, W. "The African World and The Ethnocultural Debate". *African Culture: The Rhythms of Unity.* Ed. M.K. Asante and K.W. Asante. Trenton, NJ: Africa New World Press, 1990.

Taussig, M. *Mimesis and Alterity: A Particular History of the Senses.* New York: Routledge, 1993.

Thomas, J. "Poetry fires hot Brand novel". *The Globe and Mail* June 29 (1996): C20.

Toop, D. *The Rap Attack: African Jive to New York Hip Hop.* London: Pluto Press, 1984.

Troupe, Q. *Avalanche.* Minneapolis: Coffee House Books, 1996.

Walcott, R. (1995). "'Out of the Kumbla': Toni Morrison's Jazz and Pedagogical Answerability". *Cultural Studies*, Vol.9, No.2 (1995): 318-337.

———. "'Voyage Through the Multiverse': Contested Canadian Identities". *Border/lines* 36 (1995): 49-52.

———. "Lament for a Nation: The Racial Geography of the Oh! Canada Project". *Fuse Magazine* Vol.19, No.4, (1996): 15-23.

Wallace, M. "Modernism, Postmodernism and the Problem of the Visual in Afro-American Culture". *Out There: Marginalization and Contemporary Cultures.* Ed. R. Ferguson, M. Gever, T. Minh-ha and C. West. New York: The New Museum of Contemporary Art and The MIT Press, 1990.

———. "Afterword: 'Why Are There No Great Black Artists?': The

Problem of Visuality in African-American Culture". *Black Popular Culture*. Ed. G. Dent. Seattle: Bay Press, 1992.

Watts, J. *Heroism and the Black Intellectual: Ralph Ellison, Politics, and Afro-American Intellectual Life*. Chapel Hill, NC: The University of North Carolina Press, 1994.

West, C. "The New Cultural Politics of Difference". *Out There: Marginalization and Contemporary Cultures*. Ed. R. Ferguson, M. Gever, T. Minh-ha and C. West. New York: The New Museum of Contemporary Art and The MIT Press. 1990.

White, H. "Bodies and Their Plots". *Choreographing History*. Ed. S. L. Foster. Bloomington, IN: Indiana University Press, 1995.

Winks, R. *The Blacks in Canada: A History*. Montreal and New Haven: McGill University Press and Yale University Press, 1971.

Wynter, S. "Rethinking 'Aesthetics': Notes Towards A Deciphering Practice". *Ex-Iles: Essays on Caribbean Cinema*. Ed. M. Cham. Trenton, NJ: Africa World Press, Inc., 1992.

———. "Beyond Miranda's Meanings: Un/Silencing the 'Demonic Ground' of Caliban's 'Woman'". *Out of the Kumbla: Caribbean Women and Literature*. Ed. C. Boyce-Davies and E.S. Fido. Trenton, NJ: Africa World Press, 1990.

Discography

Allen, L. *Revolutionary Tea Party*. Toronto, ON: Verse to Vinyl Records, 1985.

Devon. *It's My Nature*. Toronto, ON: Capitol Records-EMI of Canada, 1992.

Dream Warriors. *And Now the Legacy Begins*. Scarborough, ON: Island Records, 1991.

Joseph, C. "Pimps". "A Chant for Monk 3". *Oral/Trans/Missions*. Toronto, ON: Verse to Vinyl Records, 1989.

Maestro Fresh-Wes. *Naaah, Dis Kid Can't be from Canada*, Toronto, ON: Attic Records, 1994.

Soul II Soul. *Keep On Movin*. Toronto, ON: Virgin Records Canada, 1989.

Filmography

Julien, I. *Young Soul Rebels*, Miramax, 1991.

Philips, C. *Making Change*, Golchonda Media Inc., 1995.

Williams, S. *Saar*, Moving Images, 1994.

Williams, S. *Variation on a Key 2 Life*, Canadian Film Centre, 1993.

———. *Soul Survivor*, Norstar, 1995.

Virgo, C. *Save My Lost Nigga' Soul*, Canadian Film Centre, 1994.

———. *Rude*, Cineplex Odeon, 1995.

Index

Rinaldo Walcott is an assistant Professor of Humanities at York University. His research and teaching is focused in the area of black cultural studies.